Against All Odds

Robert Poku

Jesus Joy Publishing

First Published and printed in Great Britain in 2019 by Jesus Joy Publishing.

© Robert Poku, 2019

Scripture Quotations

ISBN 978-1-90797-162-4

Jesus Joy Publishing

a division of Eklegein Ltd

www.jesusjoypublishing.co.uk

20102019

Dedication

I dedicate this book to God - for His everlasting mercy and loving-kindness towards me.

Acknowledgements

First of all, I would like to express my gratitude to the Lord Almighty for providing me with the inspiration and the ability to write this book. If He had not been on my side, I would not have been able to finish it.

I would also like to thank Pastor Paul James, Senior Pastor of Harrow International Christian Centre for his spiritual guidance and inspiration in my life. I would like to extend my thanks to the following people: Evangelist Alex Osei and Dr Albert Okoye for their prayer support. I am very appreciative of Rev. Eddy Owusu, Rev. Elliot Asiedu, Rev. Samuel Akoto and Rev. Alex Boachie who stood by me during turbulent times in my life.

I would also like to thank Rev. Eric Aidoo, Rev. Edward Poku, Rev. Steven Addo, and Rev. Adu Wusu, for their support in prayers.

I give many thanks to Chalmers Poku, Rev. Charles

Saforo and Dr Isaac Addo for their involvement in the editing and proof-reading stages.

Finally and above all, I would like to give a special thank you to my wonderful wife, Naomi, and our four children - Michaela, Jesse, Jader-Elijah and Jaron-Elisha. May she be richly blessed by the Lord God for her support.

Foreword

As a friend and colleague of Robert Poku, I am delighted to endorse his third book. He draws from years of experience at the coalface of Church ministry and delivers a message that will ignite faith to believe once more for God's intervention in areas of life where faith has died.

Can events that took place in an insignificant town called Bethany 2,000 years ago impact the lives of the Christians today? The answer is Yes! And so, to approach this book as a lightweight paperback would be a mistake because it explores the hard and tough issues we all face, and is drawn from the experience of personal pain in life and ministry. Its pages unravel the story of two sisters who carry the heartbreaking loss of their brother Lazarus. It is honest about human weakness, real about suffering that life can bring and applies the Word of God with balance and accuracy.

In everyday language, Robert unpacks truth with clear application to life in a way that will cause the believer to walk in faith even when facing the trials, storms and spiritual adversaries that seek to undermine real faith in God.

Robert brings clear scriptural insight, balancing real-life issues with the revelation of the Word, and challenges the believer to break loose from the chains and grave clothes of the past, as they hear the voice of God declaring freedom through Jesus.

May all who open its pages rise to a new place in their prayer life as Robert explores the keys to walking in victory.

Pastor Paul James
Senior Minister Harrow International Christian Centre

Contents

Introduction

The life of a Christian can sometimes be ugly, unpleasant and tough, but with God, all things will turn out for His glory. The Bible declares that:

"He has made everything beautiful in its time..."

(Ecclesiastes 3:11)

The central message of this book is that God reveals His answers at the perfect time and shows the importance of accommodating patience to get a greater yield of hope. It silences all doubters of God's power and assures those waiting on His promises that His delays do not mean His denial.

Life is a battlefield, where various forms and shapes of attacks are always imminent. Our social and economic status, physical strength and age, and the fact that we are Christians or otherwise does not exempt us from being assailed by troubles.

When a young man called Lazarus in Bethany, whom Jesus loved, experienced an untimely death, it shocked many since he was the friend of a healer. He became sick, died and was buried.

Let's get this straight - even though he was loved by Jesus, that didn't prevent him from getting sick and dying. But what looked like the end of life, became a glorious moment of his destiny.

Sometimes, the righteous suffer during the events in their lives which make it seem like everything is against them. Like travelling by boat and sailing in a stormy sea, we can't avoid the boisterous wind, but we can raise or lower our sail to get to our destination safely. What is important here is not how powerful the wind is, but the way we respond to it. In response to every compelling and challenging situation that may come our way, our ability to trust, obey, and look to God in faith for direction, and wait patiently on Him to save the situation, is key.

Our afflictions may be many to the point that it

cripples all hope of survival, but we are assured of complete deliverance by our Lord Jesus and which comes in His own perfect time.

People everywhere suffer the bad things this world throws at them and many of them can barely stand against the odds. They are walking the streets with a real lack of faith about the future and no direction towards their destiny. There is an urgent need to help such people - the type of help that has no strings attached and that encourages, gives purpose and uplifts. Just look at Lazarus - Lazarus was alive, became sick, and the next day he was dead, and just four days later he was alive again. A lot can happen in a year, a month, a week and even days.

'Survival of the fittest' is a common phrase that I hear a lot, but I believe that this phrase does not apply to everyone. As Christians, we survive not because of our fitness but because our anchor is held in Jesus Christ - our solid Rock and firm foundation.

We all react differently to challenging situations; some will stand right in the firing line and hold their nerve, while some will run in fear that the odds are against them. I have faced some challenges myself and have been under attack from the enemy; but I stand to declare that with the Lord, all things are possible; and no matter how difficult the circumstances seem, there is still hope for the one who waits on God. Sometimes our prayers won't be answered immediately, but He will do it in His time.

Martha and Mary thought that the removal of the stone couldn't result in a resurrection, but it would rather cause a stench in the whole place. But against all odds, their brother Lazarus came forth instead of the expected stench. The voice of Jesus is still active and calling sinners, backsliders and the broken-hearted to come forth.

As you read this book, it is my prayer that you hold on to faith and trust the Lord during your time of trouble and perplexity, and that you understand the reason you should wait when the answer tarries. In the encouraging words of the Apostle Peter:

> *"But may the God of all grace, who called us to His eternal glory by Christ Jesus, after you have suffered a while, perfect, establish, strengthen, and settle you."*
>
> *(1 Peter 5:10, NKJV)*

Chapter One

Trouble in Bethany

When Trouble Comes

In this world, problems are inevitable and no one is exempted from having a share of their sour taste. We cannot hide from their poisonous sting; whether we turn to the left or right, we will face them. We face problems in relationships, finances and sometimes our health. The righteous man, Job, was right to state that:

> *"... man is born to trouble, as the sparks fly upward"*
>
> *(Job 5:7)*

Considering this statement of Job, you will notice that problems are common to us all and the occurrence of them is unavoidable.

Whether you are a Christian or not, you cannot be spared from the trouble that is certain to happen in your life from birth - because of sin. We should not deceive ourselves with the notion that Christians are exempted from problems as some may think. Bad things can sometimes happen to good people as often as they do to bad people. How the situation is handled is what matters and that is what distinguishes the two. Interestingly, Jesus clearly spoke about what we should expect in the world and what we should do according to the Apostle John:

> *"... things I have spoken to you, that in Me you may have peace. In the world, you will have tribulation, but be of cheer, I have overcome the world."*
>
> *(John 16:33)*

As we are all familiar with the struggles of pain and suffering, we know the need to rely on the Lord Jesus for our comfort, peace and good health. We sometimes miss out and get the opposite, but this does not mean the promise does not hold true. I believe God does not want us to be naive about the trials and tribulations that accompany a Christian lifestyle. There are many instances in a believers' life where a series of bad events occur. An example is Joseph, the son of Jacob and Rachel, who went through a series of problems before the fulfilment of his dreams when Pharaoh appointed Joseph as Prime Minister with the words:

"See, I have set you over all the land of Egypt."

(Genesis 41:41)

Let us not forget that prior to being chosen as a prime minister in Egypt, Joseph encountered a lot of problems. In fact, it was obvious from a human standpoint that Joseph would die in prison with his God-given dream. But what seemed to be a problem, became the source of his praise.

Whether you are a Christian, or otherwise, you will someday come across problems. We are not automatically entitled to have an easy ride on our Christian journey which starts from the day we accepted Christ to be our Lord and Saviour. We may experience bumpy roller-coaster rides that will have many ups and downs. There will be times that we may have to go through the darkest valleys in order to climb and overcome our mountains, times when we will break down in tears before we can gift the world with our smile. Jesus rightly encourages us to "CHEER UP", in the midst of trouble. So we should not allow the problems we face each day to draw us away from the Lord; but rather draw us to Him. As they say, *'when troubles get you, try and get Jesus'*. He has overcome the world and all its troubles, and He is too faithful to allow any kind of problems to overtake us.

A Glimmer of Hope

When someone is sick, the first question we ask is whether they have seen a doctor for medication or not. We tend to believe doctors have all the knowledge and expertise regarding our health, so we put our trust in their diagnoses and prescriptions. Their profession is such that they are there to help when you call on them, something that they are legally bound to do. However, if you are unwell, and you choose not to call or visit them, then you cannot blame them, should the worse happen.

Most people have heard about Jesus and had basic knowledge of some of His works, but they rarely choose to call on Him during their difficult moments. Some of these people may even claim to believe in Jesus but are overly concerned about what people may think when the time comes for them to totally depend on him. For Martha and Mary, they did not hesitate to break the news to Jesus and ask Him for help in their situation. According to Apostle John's account:

"... a certain man was sick, Lazarus of Bethany, the town of Mary and her sister Martha.

It was the same Mary who anointed the Lord with fragrant oil and wiped His feet with her hair, whose brother Lazarus was now sick. Therefore, the sisters sent to Him, saying, 'Lord, behold, he whom You love is sick.'"

(John 11:1-3)

The message was short and brief. The sisters knew that when it came to love, no one could love Lazarus more than Jesus and then again, that He could heal him from that particular sickness.

A certain man was sick unto death; and after all attempts from qualified physicians proved futile, his relatives decided to visit a sorcerer to find out the cause of his sickness. His children, knowing the importance of their father's faith, stepped in for him and thought it was a good idea to bring up the fact that their father believed in Jesus and that He would not like the idea of a sorcerer giving him answers.

These children 'stood in the gap' for their father with prayer and fasting instead, seeking the face of God for their father's healing and God intervened for them. Their decision paid off and miraculously the man was healed. This incident exalted the name of the Lord in the hospital and drew people to the saving knowledge of the Lord. How many times do we pray to God and stand in the gap for our loved ones who cannot do it themselves?

Do we pray and ask the Lord to save our loved ones who do not know Him, or are we too tied down asking for everything for ourselves that we forget about everybody else? We should understand that God's love is not limited to a few people and has no boundaries.

It was out of desperation and in those pressing moments, Martha and Mary made a perfect decision and were convinced that Jesus could heal their brother. Every now and then, we hear desperate voices calling and crying from broken marriages and broken homes, longing for someone who will listen to their story. If the fallen world has a problem, it means they do not know Jesus and have refused to call on Him for help. In that helpless state, Martha and Mary sent for Jesus. In a way, they stood in for their brother by calling on Jesus. The psalmist states:

> "God is our refuge and strength, A very present help in trouble."

(Psalm 46:1)

For Martha and Mary, the day of trouble had come, and so they searched for Jesus.

Our Help Comes from The Lord

At some time or another, we will all need help from someone. But sometimes, getting help from the right people can be challenging. Not everybody can lead you out of your troubles; indeed, some people can instead put you into more troubling situations. It is a misjudgement to assume that God is far away from helping us, so we therefore refuse to call on Him when problems arise.

We commonly come to the conclusion that the things we are unable to do, cannot be done at all.

Sometimes, what is letting us down is the way we exaggerate our problems making them look bigger than God and so making God our second option. We behave like we know it all, just to feed our egos, having forgotten that all of us have limitations.

"... and if anyone thinks that he knows anything, he knows nothing yet as he ought to know."

(1 Corinthians 8:2)

A woman once told me about her son who had been continuously suffering from seizures, recounting how she had visited many places hoping to get the problem solved. *"Pastor", she said, "I can't bear the sight of him chewing his tongue. Sometimes I have to put a cloth in his mouth to prevent him from endangering himself but yet, I see the cloth soaked with blood. I thought I had found a solution, not knowing I had fallen into wrong hands. I was the one drinking the concoction for my son."*

In fact, when she finished speaking, I realised that despite all her wealth and status, her desperate quest for help had landed her into wrong hands. Sometimes, out of desperation, we can also find ourselves falling into the wrong hands and become nothing but inanimate pieces on a black and white chessboard, only to be moved when the hands controlling us move us in order to complete the game of life. This generally happens, when we depend entirely on a creature in the world rather than the Creator who made all things. King Asa is a good example.

"... in the thirty-ninth year of his reign, Asa became diseased in his feet, and his malady was severe, yet in his disease, he did not seek the Lord, but the physicians."

(2 Chronicles 16:12)

The question that we have to ask ourselves is - when troubles come, what do we do? We are given two options in this situation, to either call on the Lord during our problems or rely on our own strength to carry us through. When making this decision, we should remember that *"... (my) our help comes from the Lord."* (Psalm 121)

God's Perfect Time

Let us understand, however, that there is always a light at the end of the tunnel, and the things that are supposed to bring us disgrace, by divine intervention, will be the same things that will bring us glory and the rewards that we longed for:

> *"... for I consider that the sufferings of this present time are not worthy to be compared with the glory which shall be revealed in us."*
>
> *(Romans 8:18)*

This verse explains how our suffering becomes incomparable to our rewards when we receive them, and how when we get our rewards, the suffering becomes nothing but a stepping stone. These rewards may be long in coming, and what we receive may not wholly meet our specifications. However, as Christians, our desires and expectations are not automatically scheduled to come to fruition within our own time frame. Sometimes, we have to wait a little while before our requests are answered. I totally believe in what the scripture says in Psalms:

"... for the needy shall not always be forgotten; the expectation of the poor shall not perish forever."

(Psalm 9:18)

However, in certain cases, things can turn ugly before they get better. There are times that we may lose before we gain, and cry before we smile. Let us consider how the book of Ecclesiastes puts it:

"To everything there is a season, a time for every purpose under heaven."

(Ecclesiastes 3:1)

I have realised that sometimes the things that look like they may destroy you in one particular season, will rather serve to prepare you well for the next.

One day my car developed a mechanical fault and I sent it to my mechanic to fix it. In fact, I had a meeting, and from the way I saw things, I would be late if the problem was not dealt with immediately. After some time, the mechanic told me I may have to wait an hour before the problem could be fixed. I did not like this idea of waiting but I realised that the best option was to reach my destination late than to get a breakdown in the middle of the road and not reach my destination at all.

A Message to The Lord

When Martha and Mary sent a message to Jesus, he did not decline the invitation to visit Lazarus and neither did he follow up immediately. Rather, he tarried for two days. (John 11:6) Only Jesus knows why we sometimes do not get an instant response when we pray. Why should we have to wait for today's answer tomorrow? He even spoke to His disciples that this sickness would not end in death:

"This sickness is not unto death, but for the glory of God, that the Son of God may be glorified through it.

(John 11:4)

After this statement, Jesus said, *"Lazarus has fallen asleep; I am going there to wake him up."* (John 11:11)

However, the story changed in verse 14 when the disciples having misunderstood Him were told plainly, that Lazarus was dead. Whether we like it or not, things may not go our way and against all odds, the unexpected or feared outcome could happen.

There will be the times when our faith will be stretched and exhausted. A time will come when you will have to shift your focus from the problem and rely on Jesus for an explanation. But what we must keep in mind, is that an unexpected delay will be part of our story and could even be a vital part of our testimonies.

Now the reality of Lazarus' sickness had been

unfolded to the disciples, and at that time, they may have asked why Jesus was not under pressure by the expectation of everyone for Him to fix Lazarus' problem.

Let us be mindful of the way we approach God in our dark moments. As a result of our situation, we allow ourselves to become a flurry of uncontrollable emotions and believe the silence of God shows His refusal to answer our prayers. This is when some of us start to question why He said He loved us. Let us remember that Jesus is not our 'Client'; He is our Redeemer and Saviour - the One who understands our battles and struggles. We may not know how and when He will fix our problems, but that is down to Him and His judgement. Let us remember that He told the disciples earlier *"I Am Going To Wake Him Up"*. It means that He has the ultimate answer for Lazarus, even though He had delayed His visit. He knows our hearts' desire before we even ask of Him. He exhorts us:

"Therefore do not be like them. For your Father knows the things you have need of before you ask Him."

(Matthew 6:8)

In Pursuit of the Saviour

There were times in my life when I faced a swift rush of multiple challenges. I saw issues that I could handle and also realised what I could not do even as a child of God. As a matter of fact, I sought and waited on the Lord during those moments for strength. During those periods, I kept my prayer life alive, constantly holding on to the promises of God. I learned how the Apostle Paul, in one of his letters, is glad to talk about the grace Jesus showed upon him in his time of weakness. He states:

"... lest I should be exalted above measure by the abundance of the revelations, a thorn in the flesh was given to me, a messenger of Satan to buffet me, lest I be exalted above measure. Concerning this

thing I pleaded with the Lord three times
that it might depart from me. And He said
to me, 'My grace is sufficient for you, for My
strength is made perfect in weakness.'
Therefore most gladly I will rather boast in
my infirmities, that the power of Christ may
rest upon me. Therefore I take pleasure in
infirmities, in reproaches, in needs, in
persecutions, in distresses, for Christ's sake.
For when I am weak, then I am strong."

(2 Corinthians 12:7-10)

Anyone who has suffered or has had a 'thorn in the flesh' experience, will tell of how, in those moments, our faith is stretched to its limits.

Imagine a life filled with pain that is not ready to go, sickness not responding to treatment. Waking up with a 'hangover of pains', the nightmare of your yesterday constantly breathing down your neck in the dawn of each new day, just another haunting reminder of where you have been defeated. Something we rarely forget, are the flashbacks of upsetting events. Horrible events always seem to remain in our long-term memory, acting as an alarm to remind us of our past failures, and what we cannot do in the future. Despite these little reminders, we rarely stop to consider how fortunate we truly are compared to those who have their lives totally bombarded with struggles and do not know the Lord. This brings me to a common saying when things do not work to suit our needs - 'life is just not fair'. We look for respite, and faith in order to persevere, discarding anything that proves to be an obstacle.

The advantage we have, as Christians, however, is that we are gifted with the knowledge of the Lord, and can call upon Him through prayer when our storms of trouble come. God declares:

> *"Call upon Me in the day of trouble; I will deliver you, and you shall glorify Me."*
>
> *(Psalm 50:15)*

Jesus Our Ultimate Helper

Now, the two sisters, Mary and Martha, had one person in mind whom they could rely on. They sat at His feet and observed his lifestyle, and His deeds attested to the fact that He was indeed a healer. He was the one of whom Isaiah said:

> *"The Spirit of the Lord God is upon Me, Because the Lord has anointed Me to preach good tidings to the poor; He has sent Me to heal the broken-hearted, to proclaim liberty to the captives, and the opening of the prison to those who are bound."*
>
> *(Isaiah 61:1)*

We often find ourselves compelled to pray daily for strength and protection, inquiring of God to deploy His angels to protect us. If we find ourselves lacking the help and provisions of God, we are more prone to increased vulnerability and exposure to trouble. There are people in our lives, however, who are capable of doing many things for us when we are in need, to help us to maintain serenity in our hearts. Despite this, their attempt to re-establish peace in your life is, in a way, limited. The trouble you are facing is a locked door which they can partly see through, but do not have the key to open. When darkness overshadows you, light is what you need to lead you out. It is like being trapped in a dark cave or tunnel and having that undisputed light as your guide to safety. When we see Jesus as our ultimate Saviour and Redeemer, our life will no longer be continuously overwhelmed by today's troubles. Even if they do, the strength of the Lord will lift our troubles off our shoulders and will help us overcome them.

Why Should We Look unto Jesus in Our Troubled Times?

There are four Characteristics of God which are helpful to recall because it gives us abundant hope when trouble comes.

- His Mercy

- His Compassion

- His Faithfulness

- He Is Our Portion

His Mercy

Our hope in life is built on nothing else but the unmerited mercies of God. Our pleas do not fall onto deaf ears for He is the One who does not sleep nor slumber for our sake; neither are we consumed by the never-ending misery of this present life. This we can call to mind - that we have been served something we did not work for or deserve. Now we can encourage ourselves in Him and stay hopeful when trouble comes.

The Bible also reminds us of the following:

"Blessed be the God and Father of our Lord Jesus Christ, who according to His abundant mercy has begotten us again to a living hope through the resurrection of Jesus Christ from the dead."

(1 Peter 1:3)

"'This I recall to my mind, therefore I have hope. Through the Lord's mercies we are not consumed, because His compassions fail not. They are new every morning; great is Your faithfulness. The Lord is my portion,' says my soul, 'Therefore I hope in Him!'"

(Lamentations 3:21-24)

His Compassion

We are fortunate to enjoy the unending love of God. It does not run out and is renewed every morning. Just imagine Jesus reminding you to relax after all the wailing and sleepless nights you have had and saying, *'I have been through the same, so I know how to lead you through.'* Jesus has been in the same conditions as us and experienced the same feelings.

"Knowing then that we have a great High Priest who has passed through the heavens, Jesus the Son of God, let us hold fast our confession. For we do not have a High Priest who cannot sympathise with our

weaknesses but was in all points tempted
as we are, yet without sin. Let us therefore
come boldly to the throne of grace, that we
may obtain mercy and find grace to help in
time of need."

(Hebrews 4:14-16)

His Faithfulness

My mother often went to the hospital to undergo frequent health checks. There was a particular doctor that she did not want to miss any time she visited. He was punctual with time and duty, and He made time for his patients and took good care of them. One day the unexpected happened. My mum went for her usual check up and to her surprise, the doctor she trusted had had a stroke and had been bed bound. As good and caring as he was, on that day my mother met with disappointment. She had trusted him to the point that when it turned out that he could not help her on that day, she was disappointed. Who do you trust enough that you are assured that they cannot disappoint you? The reality is, that no one except God has the ability to help us continuously without disappointment. He is too faithful to fail and disappoint us. It is in God's highest interest to keep His promises.

Further Scriptures

"Therefore let those who suffer according to the will of God commit their souls to Him in doing good, as to a faithful Creator."

(1 Peter 4:19)

"God is faithful, by whom you were called into the fellowship of His Son, Jesus Christ our Lord."

(1 Corinthians 1:9)

"No temptation has overtaken you except such as is common to man; but God is faithful, who will not allow you to be tempted beyond what you are able, but with the temptation will also make the way of escape, that you may be able to bear it."

(1 Corinthians 10:13)

"But the Lord is faithful, who will establish you and guard you from the evil one."

"If we are faithless, He remains faithful; He cannot deny Himself."

(2 Timothy 2:13)

"Let us hold fast the confession of our hope without wavering, for He who promised is faithful."

(Hebrews 10:23)

"God is faithful, by whom you were called into the fellowship of His Son, Jesus Christ our Lord."

(1 Corinthians 1:9)

"Therefore know that the Lord your God, He is God, the faithful God who keeps covenant and mercy for a thousand generations with those who love Him and keep His commandments."

(Deuteronomy 7:9)

He Is Our Portion

There are dangers in making God our second option. We have no right as Christians to put our faith in any other god when they seem to have an immediate solution to our problems. Many people want things fixed within their own time frame, and so they do not realise the consequences that may come their way.

King Saul was a prime example and a sober warning to us all:

> *"So Saul died for his unfaithfulness which he had committed against the Lord, because he did not keep the word of the Lord, and also because he consulted a medium for guidance."*
>
> *(1 Chronicles 10:13)*

I have that which is sufficient to balance all my troubles and make up for all my losses. For, while portions on earth are empty and perishing things, God is an all-sufficient and durable portion, a portion forever. As long as we continue to serve and seek Him, God will satisfy our needs. Therefore, I will hope in Him — I will trust in Him and encourage myself in Him when all other sources of support and encouragement fail me.

We can live in this world with the assurance that our portion is not kept in the earthly realm, but that the One who made and governs the world is our sole portion. The Lord's portion, unlike any in this world, is infinite, and with it, comes the inheritance of the Kingdom of Heaven:

> *"My flesh and my heart fail; But God is the strength of my heart and my portion forever."*
>
> *(Psalm 73:26)*

Chapter Two

Jesus in Bethany

Jesus Is Never Late

It is possible to allow doubts to build up in our minds, thinking that God is too far from helping us. However, if we call on God when pressure mounts, and exercise patience during our waiting period, we shall surely enjoy His glory. A lot of Christians are impatient and are anxious about how God will answer their prayers. Though it costs to wait, but those who wait and fear the Lord shall never be disappointed:

> *"Behold, the eye of the Lord is on those who fear Him, On those who hope in His mercy, To deliver their soul from death, And to keep them alive in famine. Our soul waits for the Lord; He is our help and our shield. For our heart shall rejoice in Him, Because we have trusted in His holy name."*
>
> *(Psalm 33:18-21)*

Now within the period of time that Jesus knew Lazarus was sick, to the time He arrived in town, there was a moment of shock and anxiety. A period of heartbreak for Martha and Mary; as their hopes to see Jesus when their brother was sick faded. The only person they could trust to heal their brother Lazarus did not come and He did not send any message of hope either.

At one time or another, we have all experienced such a telling moment in our life. We have prayed about something and yet heaven remains still and silent when we needed to take a 'quick' decision in that situation.

This is a perfect ground for doubt to thrive. We think to ourselves, 'Have my prayers gone unnoticed?', 'Will my prayers be left unanswered?' Some of us like to call these difficult times, the silent period': periods where we think that God doesn't care and has, in fact, forgotten about us. Any time these questions come to my mind, I always respond with my knowledge of the fact that God has never been late and does not intend to keep us in suspense. How many of us would go to the hospital and do our own surgery just because the doctor is taking longer than we expected? No matter the severity of the injury, my guess is that all of us would wait for the doctor because they are professionals who know what to do to help us. When we tell God our problems, let us remain patient, sit in the waiting room, and wait until He is ready to visit us and solve them.

Normally when we ask God for something, in prayer, and the opposite happens, our instincts tell us not to pray any more. Most of the time, we see our problems as *'too big for God to solve'*; so we undermine His power, and therefore allow the enemy to give us different options to get a quick solution to what we ask for.

Because we think that God is too far away to help us, we also tend to ignore His presence. I know many Christians who have 'back up' plans in case

God does not come through for them in the way they wanted Him to. I do not call it a 'back up' plan; I call it 'self-help'. We are doing something without involving the Lord. This mindset can be mostly seen in the 'new age' movement where the belief is that doing things our own way is the best way to go. Any time we run out of patience, we ignore God's promises and do things our way. We should not set timelines for God no matter the situation in our walk with Him. God told the prophet, Habakkuk:

> *"... though it tarry, wait for it; because it will surely come, it will not tarry."*
>
> *(Habakkuk 2:3)*

Even though Jesus delayed in coming to see Lazarus, He was never going to be late in executing His plans.

All Possible Threats Are Overruled By Jesus

There is no easy road to any accomplishment. Certainly, there will be some setbacks, battles to be fought and decisions to be made. Bethany was not safe for Jesus and his disciples; as a matter of fact, there were some concerns about Jesus' plans to go there, as the Jews had attempted to stone Him when He visited before. The disciples said to Him:

> *"Rabbi, lately the Jews sought to stone You,*
> *and are You going there again?"*
>
> *(John 11:8)*

As each day has its own set of challenges and troubles, we see how sometimes our faith turns into fear and our strength turned into a weakness.

The disciples were very disturbed by the perceived danger ahead of them in Judea, nevertheless, Jesus was in no way perturbed. He was more concerned about the state of Lazarus and his sisters and for that matter, ignored all possible threats. We fail to understand and sometimes forget that Christians are on the front-line in battle, fighting principalities, demons and evil spirits which tend to resist every move we make:

*"Therefore we wanted to come to you -
even I, Paul, time and again - but Satan
hindered us."*

(1 Thessalonians 2:18)

We must admit that God has given us Jesus Christ, our Lord, to champion the course of our journey. God knows all the possible traps and dangers the enemy has put in our way, but this means nothing when Jesus leads the way.

Jesus knew that Martha and Mary were filled with sorrow and grief after losing their only brother. Nothing hurts more than losing a dear one; an irreplaceable object. Even though Jesus knew the imminent threats of the Jews against Him, He ignored it and therefore carried out his visit for He loved the family. The Apostle John recalls Jesus' words:

*"Greater love has no one than this, than to
lay down one's life for his friends."*

(John 15:13)

I am yet to find someone who is willing to lay

down his or her life in exchange for the lives of others in the name of love. Jesus can and He did. He said:

> *"I am the good shepherd. The good shepherd gives His life for the sheep."*
>
> *(John 10:11)*

Relatively speaking, Jesus, our Good Shepherd, will not desert us when troubles come. He understands the kind of let-down and betrayal from our bosom friends.

Panic In The Face Of Uncertainty

Occasionally, we grumble feeling distressed considering the magnitude of the situation especially when we say yes to the work of God. I have learned from experience that problems come in different shapes and forms. Like the storms, we cannot stop it, but we can adjust our sail. One day, I was travelling to Dallas, Texas for a programme. The journey was smooth at the beginning until we experienced some turbulence. In fact, the turbulence was so severe that any possibility of reaching our destination was out of the question. My mind was troubled and reeled with worry. Without hesitation, I began to pray to invoke the name of Jesus. A lady sitting beside me began to mention the name of Jesus too. She had her earphones on listening to music, but she pulled them off and decided to face the situation by appealing to Jesus. Nobody told us to scream the name of Jesus, the turbulence did. I looked at the situation and I realised how a bad situation can reveal what you believe in. Maybe if someone stood up to preach Jesus, he would have been asked to be silent but to my surprise nobody did.

Who is your anchor during your troubled times? Having your anchor firmly placed in God means that you do not need to worry because He is our Solid Rock; all you have to do is trust in Him. When everything has settled down and the turbulence had stopped, the whole plane breathed a sigh of relief as we realised, we were spared from death. I could not let this evangelical opportunity slip away so I started to talk about

Jesus Christ to this young lady. When our souls are troubled and we are overwhelmed, that is the best moment to seek Jesus.

When my soul is troubled and I see no life but death, I will give the Lord my attention. I observed one thing during that terrible ordeal, we all calmed down when the pilot reassured us that we would be fine. As I sat down on my seat reflecting on the pilot's words of assurance, this was what I saw even in the midst of the turbulence - everybody gave their attention to the pilot and stopped screaming. When this near-death situation was over, life on the plane returned to normal. We were all humbled thinking how this would be our end.

The young lady sitting next to me made her statement afterwards, *"I must start going to church."* I said to her, *"... don't wait another moment for turbulence to arise again before you start seeking the Lord."* I did not want her to waste any more chances in her life and redirected her towards the Lord's path. Indeed, there will be difficulties but as long as we trust and hold on to Jesus, we will make it.

Jesus Came to Saves Us

Martha and Mary were notable for their hospitality and the services they had rendered to our Lord Jesus. But they were not spared the suffering of the excruciating pain over the loss of their brother, Lazarus. According to a Nigerian proverb,

"When the roots of a tree begin to decay, it spreads death to the branches."

The death of a loved one can affect us in many ways. It can create an emotional and psychological imbalance in our lives. It has no respect for anyone, and it can literally visit unexpectedly. It entered Bethany, picked Lazarus as one of its victims, wrapped its icy arms around him and took him away. But Jesus eventually arrived at Bethany even though His arrival was considered delayed by the sisters. However, His delay did not stop Him from doing what He wanted to do. He made a request to see the dead man, Lazarus.

To help us understand the mission of Christ and what He came on earth to do, let us read what the prophet Isaiah said about Him:

> *"The Spirit of the Lord God is upon Me, Because the Lord has anointed Me To preach good tidings to the poor; He has sent Me to heal the broken-hearted, To proclaim liberty to the captives, And the opening of the prison to those who are bound."*
>
> *(Isaiah 61:1)*

I strongly believe that Jesus, through the Holy Spirit, is on a mission to pick us up from any horrible state. We can be walking in the valley of the shadow of death and be afraid, but even in these darkest places, the Good Shepherd will come to our rescue:

"... you will not abandon me to the realm of the dead, nor will you let your faithful one see decay."

(Psalm16:10, NIV)

This is our confidence - that He has assured us He has a deep connection with all of His children who are kept even unto death. He knows the danger that His stray sheep can encounter. The Prophet Ezekiel also said:

"As a shepherd seeks out his flock on the day he is among his scattered sheep, so will I seek out My sheep and deliver them from all the places where they were scattered on a cloudy and dark day."

(Ezekiel 34:12)

Jesus, being the Good Shepherd, does not only look for the lost sheep which are still alive, He protects, preserves and delivers those who are dying as well. John records Jesus as stating:

"This is the will of the Father who sent Me, that of all He has given Me I should lose

nothing, but should raise it up at the last day. And this is the will of Him who sent Me, that everyone who sees the Son and believes in Him may have everlasting life; and I will raise him up at the last day."

It is within the power of Jesus to seek those that are lost and save them. The problems of yesterday, today and those to come are not too big for the Lord. No problem is too big for Jesus and His ability to solve our problems is unparalleled. There is no better re-assurance than this - *"Jesus Christ is the same yesterday and today and forever."* (Hebrews 13:8)

Where Have You Laid Him?

Now, the day was no longer bright and fair in the town of Bethany but was overshadowed by the darkness caused by death. The relatives of Lazarus had given him a ceremonial burial. Actually, it was the moment of giving a final farewell to the deceased. People were wailing and crying; amongst them was Jesus, our Great Comforter, who could not hide His emotions. He wept on that occasion.

Jesus had a different view of the situation. He understands our pilgrimage through the horrible pits, valleys and mountains we climb in our everyday life. We should be careful not to settle down in a desirable and pleasant place, thinking that a life lived in the dark valleys is to be avoided at all costs. Jesus comes to us and says *'take me in there'* to these areas so that He can go to the heart of the problem and solve it. He loves us so much that He always wants us to overcome our fears.

Actually, where the family members saw death and the grave, Jesus saw life and a chance for regeneration. In fact, where they saw despair and death, Jesus saw hope. Being consumed with power and love He asked them,

"'Where have you laid him?' They said to

Him, 'Lord, come and see.'"

The question Jesus asked still resonates in my mind, "... *where have you laid him?*" In other words, show me where you have buried Him - the one that "*I love*". All of us, at some point, have laid our 'LAZARUS' down to rest for a period of days, months or years. We all have a 'Lazarus' that could not survive the challenges and the perils of life, and as a result, died.

Our Lazarus could be the problems we could not fix. You have witnessed the transition - it all started with a minor problem; the problem gradually progressed and got worse and worse, and now it cannot be fixed; it is dead.

Where have you buried your 'Lazarus'? There are so many 'burial grounds' surrounding us and theoretically, they are not places where we enjoy visiting. They are found where we bury our hopes, dreams and relationships. Some of us do not want to revisit these kinds of places in order to remain within our comfort zone. And surprisingly, this is the exact place Jesus chose to visit.

There are some places that still bring back painful memories for me. Seasons have come and gone but I still cannot erase them from my mind. I remember the day my younger brother died, and we had to go to a cemetery to bury him there. The place had an aura of grief and permanent loss. The reality of death seemed to show itself every step I took as the body of my younger brother was being carried to his grave. What I could feel taking its place, was an emotional wall being built up, brick by brick, between me and any form of happiness or joy.

This trauma is similar to that which I saw in my mother, who was so distraught, that she could not even make it to the cemetery. The shock of her son's death was too much for her to bear. I was quite young at the time, but I witnessed everything that went on. From the time they carried his lifeless body to when they laid him down and covered him with sand - I saw it all. In a space of time that seemed to span only a few seconds, my brother was gone. I could not bear the agony of leaving that place without him.

One day, I was going to meet a friend and it so happened that to get there, I had to pass through the same place my brother was buried. In fact, because of the pain that the cemetery had caused me, I decided to look elsewhere when passing to avoid the site of the grave that held my loved one. I was with some friends at the time and one of them, who knew my brother, asked me this, *"... show me where your brother was buried."* Tears welled up in my eyes and I started to cry. It was because I was remembering the good times I had enjoyed with him and how now he had become history. One memory that remains in my mind, is the day he gave his life to Jesus. He saw the light, and from the darkness, he was once in, he became a new man. He changed his route, from the wavering, wide path, to the straight, narrow road. Despite feeling sad when pondering my brother's death, I know that because of that decision he made on that day, he can live eternally with the joy of the Lord.

This reminds me of the wisdom in the book of Psalms:

> *"Lord, make me to know my end, and what is the measure of my days, that I may know how frail I am."*
>
> *(Psalm 39:4)*

We will never know the exact moment we will depart from this earth, and do not know what the future holds in store. Therefore, let us cling desperately the hope of our salvation through the confession of Christ as Lord, and use it as a guide on how to live righteously until the end.

Lord, Come and See ...

When Jesus asked Martha and Mary where Lazarus had been buried, they were willing to show Him where He was. They said to Jesus, *"Come and See."* Come and see our dead brother

Lazarus, where we have laid him. Are you willing, as Christians, to allow Jesus into your broken homes and estranged relationships? Can you take Him to where you gave up and allow Him to take full control? Nothing can be done perfectly without Christ; Indeed, the statement rings true - *"Christ in me the hope of glory."* (Colossians 1:27) Our own judgements and decisions will only take us up to a certain point, and then we will see how much we depend on Christ. Who is qualified to give you the final verdict? Maybe many people have seen your situation and have given their negative opinions, so you choose not to revisit it again. We should not hesitate to show Jesus our mess and allow Him to clean it up because He is too faithful to fail us when we depend on Him.

He delights in hearing our humble prayers and then perfects whatever concerns us. He has never taken his eyes off us, even in our moments of unbelief and anxiety. He still encourages us during our worse moments by urging us to "Just Believe".

This reminds me of a story in the Gospel of Luke, Jairus was a leader of the synagogue, and his daughter was sick to death. He looked for Jesus and invited him to come to his house and heal his daughter. After a little while, someone came from his house and reported that his daughter was now dead and therefore he should not bother Jesus anymore.

> *"While He was still speaking, someone came from the ruler of the synagogue's house, saying to him, 'Your daughter is dead. Do not trouble the Teacher.' But when Jesus heard it, He answered him, saying, 'Do not be afraid; only believe, and she will be made well.'"*
>
> *(Luke 8:49-50)*

Apparently, the phrase she is dead, did not put Jesus off from honouring Jairus's invitation to see his sick daughter whether dead or alive. It is better to allow God to evaluate every situation of ours before we make any judgement.

One day my electric cooker developed a fault. My wife told me that she could not use it anymore because there was a problem with it. We bought a new one and invited an expert to come and fix the old one. When he was disconnecting the old cooker, he paused for a minute and he said to me, *"Pastor this cooker is not spoiled, it can be repaired."* He put some wires together and to my surprise, the cooker started working again. If it was not for that electrician, I would have thrown that cooker away.

I had prematurely condemned it and in a few minutes of it being repaired, it had become valuable and useful again. We tend to throw items like these away because, by our judgement, they are of no value and serve no purpose to our lives. I am guilty of throwing away a lot of things I thought were not useful anymore and later regretted the decision. Normally, we keep things that are reliable and useful as opposed to things that are broken, not working and useless. Despite this, it is not everything that stops working that should be instantly thrown away. The fact that you cannot repair it does not mean that it can never be repaired. All it takes is someone trained to repair these broken things to be used again. This is the same in our lives. We need somebody trained to repair the broken things that we have abandoned. This trained person is Jesus.

Trusting When Everything Seems Impossible

Every one of us will experience or have experienced a day where nothing seems to go well. Everything appears to be crumbling around you, leaving you in the mood of despondency. There are moments where we face mountains which become too difficult to climb. We carry burdens that become too difficult to bear and leave us with a dilemma.

We are regularly walking through the valley of dead souls, with no chance to see any line of **hope**. However, sometimes God will cause us to pass through this kind of valley to evaluate our judgement. Do we instantly give up on things that look useless on the outside when passing through these valleys? In these situations, I believe that the majority of us will experience our biggest fears and limitations; but as we wrestle with doubts in this situation, we must try to look at things from God's perspective.

I now understand the response the prophet Ezekiel gave to the **dry bones:**

> *"Then He caused me to pass by them all around, and behold, there were very many in the open valley; and indeed they were very dry. And He said to me, 'Son of man, can these bones live?'"*

> *(Ezekiel 37:2-3)*

We have all been to a place where we do not see any sign of hope. It is like everything has been cut off from reality. The blind side of our existence where we rarely find the answers to our questions. Just look at the response that Ezekiel gave, *"O Lord God, You know."* The Prophet looked at the dry bones with the eyes of the flesh and saw nor hope. He saw no destiny, purpose and no hope. He was probably saying to the Lord - how can this be? You know they are all dead and they are not coming back to life. If we compare the story of Lazarus to that of Ezekiel standing in the valley of dry bones, we can clearly see no indication of **hope** in both cases. These examples, although in the times of the Bible, are no different from what we face in our everyday life. Whether it is happening to a Christian or non-Christian, we will all be put through tests and will have to do our best to endure them.

Chapter Three

Ray of hope in Bethany

Keep Your Hope Alive, It's Not Over Yet

The perception that Christians are immune to suffering, pain and the pressures of life is false. A classic question that I hear from people is - *'If God is all-loving, why does He allow suffering in the world?'* It is sad that we are quick to question the works of God and forget to search the Bible for our difficult answers. It is our manual for life so whenever we disregard it, we will find it difficult to fix our problems and everything may look impossible.

What a counsel we often forfeit when we play down the Word of the Lord and follow our feelings! If by our actions and deeds we prevent God from being our Lord and Saviour, we are bound to have many unanswered questions related to life.

There is wisdom in the statement that, I came

across the Bible Scripture:

"Hope deferred makes the heart sick"

(Proverbs 13:12)

I came across this when all sources of help I needed seemed elusive. My left leg, for some reason, had become swollen. I had done all the blood tests and taken other necessary actions, but nothing seemed to reveal what was actually wrong. In fact, at night this pain would start so severely, that I had to engage myself in prayers just to distract my mind from it. But, the more I thought about it, the more worried I became. As a matter of fact, I realised how we can wrestle with anxiety as Christians. The only hope that I had was in the Lord because the doctors had not given me any tangible solutions.

Even though God healed me later on, I must be honest, there was this constant panic undermining my anchor of hope held with the Lord. The question that kept coming was, *"How long, O Lord?"* I can attest to the fact that what happened to me came to stir my hope in the Lord and my passion to pray blossomed out of the severe pain. I was reminded of the fact that:

> *"... we have access by faith into this grace in which we stand, and rejoice in hope of the glory of God. And not only that, but we also glory in tribulations, knowing that tribulation produces perseverance; and perseverance, character; and character, hope."*

(Romans 5:2-5)

What was meant to hurt me, rather built my hope and confidence in the Lord. Let us "count it all joy" when our problems lead us to get closer to the Lord.

If You Had Been Here

We often enjoy the blessings of life for so long, that when it is no more, we are left in a state of agony and confusion. Sometimes, frustration, fear and unbelief drive us to question the divinity of God. We often cry out - *"Lord, you better come now or never come at all.*" These are some of the statements of a faithless generation who claim to worship God but cannot trust Him. A lot of Christians do praise the Lord, testify about His goodness when things go well and blame God when it does not go their way. Probably, we trust Him more for what He did for us in the past than what He could do in the present.

Martha was so caught up in the past, she could not discern how unsearchable and untraceable the Lord's ways can be. She said to Jesus:

> *"Lord, if You had been here, my brother would not have died."*
>
> (John 11:21)

Logically, what Martha said was right; but let us not limit ourselves only to that notion. Even though His presence matters, trusting in the Word of the Lord will eventually yield the expected result that we long for.

If we can understand the omnipresence of God and the potency of the Word, we would not trek from crusade to crusade in search of miracles. Matthew brecords the words of the centurion:

"Lord, I am not worthy that You should come under my roof. But only speak a word, and my servant will be healed."

(Matthew 8:8)

The Jesus you met yesterday has not changed; He still remains the same unto you today. Although nHe did not visit His friend Lazarus when he was sick and neither came for his burial, there was a reason. Can you imagine the thoughts of all the disciples and friends when they met at Bethany, and Lazarus wasn't there but dead? They probably thought his death could have been averted if Jesus had been there. We must never forget that nothing can separate us from the love of Christ, not even death. He will always be there for us in every circumstance of life.

The Bible makes it clear, that if we call, God will answer, and while we are still speaking, He hears us (Isaiah 65:24). How awesome it is to see Jesus come to us during our tough times and tells us, *"I know your pains and your suffering for which you prayed for deliverance long ago?"* But sometimes we cast the blame and criticise, looking at the urgency of the matter, thinking that an immediate response is just what we need. Jesus had good plans for His friend so he was not worried because He knew the lesson and the glory that would come afterwards:

> *"Then Jesus said to them plainly, 'Lazarus is dead, and I am glad for your sakes that I was not there, that you may believe. Nevertheless let us go to him.'"*
>
> *(John 11:14-15)*

There shall be a Rising Up

There is a common saying that *'Everybody needs somebody'*. Those who are down need a person to tell them *"you can rise again"*.

> *"When men are cast down, then thou shalt say, There is lifting up; and he shall save the*

humble person."

(Job 22:29 KJV)

I believe there is the sound of prophetic wind blowing in this end time prompting us to arise as Christians and shine: a season of revival where the power of God shall refresh all weak believers. At that moment of mourning in Bethany, what Martha and Mary needed was strength and comfort. They knew there would be another chance to see their brother again at the resurrection on the last day. But Jesus gave a perfect statement *"Your brother will rise again."* (John 11:23) These encouraging words outlined Jesus' plans at Bethany, and also showed the family that He had a purpose for the Lazarus though he waas dead.

Because Jesus died for us, life can now be brought to perfection. Death does not have any power over us anymore; Jesus has the power of resurrection. He has the power to create and destroy, and no word from Him will ever go unaccomplished. Often, however, we are unable to understand the deep things of God, so we lose hope. But regardless of the depths of despair in which we find ourselves, there is hope.

> *"God is not a man, that He should lie, nor a son of man, that He should repent. Has He said, and will He not do? Or has He spoken, and will He not make it good."*
>
> *(Numbers 23:19)*

No matter how bad our situation may be, Jesus, our ultimate helper is beckoning us to come to Him for rest. Who does not need a time to rest? We can all admit that the world is full of troubles, troubles at home; troubles on our streets. These troubles tire us day by day and so we all long for some rest. God promised:

> *"Look, I am with you, and I will watch over you wherever you go, and I will bring you back to this land. For I will not leave you until I have done what I have promised*

you."

(Genesis 28:15)

We are fortunate to have this invitation from our Lord when we feel let down by life and restless. But sometimes we are too quick to limit God to what He can do and therefore refuse to co-operate with him. We are too tired to reach out to Him and trust Him with our problems. There are times that the problems we face seem to cause us to misunderstand God and the events going on in our lives. We want Jesus to solve these problems, but we do not know how and when He will do it. Jesus' explanation to Peter rings true for us today:

"What I am doing you do not understand
now, but you will know after this."

(John 13:7)

However, to be able to understand what God is doing, we will need to do away with every human concept and put our trust in Him. Let us not choose to lean on our own understanding, otherwise, we will not see the glory of the Lord.

Take Away The Stone

As Christians we are bound to face a series of challenges. As part of our Christian pilgrimage, there will be unpleasant circumstances and trials that will come our way. Whether we are ready or not, they are bound to come. The way we see these challenges are entirely different from the way God sees them. Let us look at the stone placed on Lazarus's tomb. To some extent it was a big issue, especially for the sisters. After giving their brother a fitting burial, they could no longer be with him. Even if Jesus had a plan, it should not be have been after he had been dead for four days.

When Jesus was led to the tomb, He saw an obstacle - a stone - that needed to be removed at that very moment. The stone, used to cover the entrance of the tomb now stood as a hindrance to Jesus. This stone shut down every hope of Lazarus returning back to life. It was the partition that separated the dead from the living, faith from doubts; but when the hour of favour came, what was meant to close down every opportunity, became a great opening.

Whatever has blocked your way as you have engaged yourself in prayer, will eventually give way to your miracle. There are so many entrances blocked by 'stones' - obstacles created by us ourselves and sometimes our loved ones.

These kinds of human-made obstacles have kept some of our destiny helpers away. They stand in the way of our salvation and glory. They become barriers to our source of help. Lazarus had now become a victim of one of these problems. Surprisingly, Jesus did not regard the stone as just another ordinary object that is associated with a burial, but rather a hindrance.

Just as a bird in a beautiful cage is limited to space in the cage, when the door enclosing the bird is opened, it can have the freedom to spread its wings and fly. Similarly when Jesus found the tomb, his friend Lazarus was under the grip of death. Now Lazarus was considered as a 'loss'; his vision and purpose had come to an end. But when God wills that you should live, even death will take its grips off you. Even when we may not understand what God is doing, and the reasons for it, we should remain obedient and believe in Him to the end. In the midst of the weeping and mourning, Jesus asked the family to do the most unusual thing - to remove the stone from the entrance of the tomb. I believe most of us do believe in God, but the problem is we rarely understand Him.

Some of the people went to mourn alongside the sisters, but it was only Jesus that saw what needed to be taken away. This is because He sees what we do not see and has the ability to change the circumstance related to life. Jesus made a request *"Take away the stone."* (John 11:39) In fact, this request raised a major concern with Martha and Mary because to them, the hope for their brother to come back to life was an illusion. They had been infected by the outbreak of the 'mourning epidemic' from those who did not know much about Jesus. Whenever we want to see a miracle performed, we must play down any human intellect and follow God's divine order. The things people say, what we come across and the type of words we hear can sometimes shut the door on our hope.

Lost In Doubts

We all have question marks in our heads. Where is the hope for Lazarus now? This is a question the family must have been asking when they saw Jesus arrive. Knowing that Lazarus, their brother, had been dead for four days, meant that a deep level of faith was needed in the lives of Martha and Mary to obey and comply with Jesus. No matter how religious you are, your faith will be tested through trials and challenges. As the Scripture states:

"My brethren, count it all joy when you fall into various trials, knowing that the testing of your faith produces patience. But let

patience have its perfect work, that you
may be perfect and complete, lacking
nothing. If any of you lacks wisdom, let him
ask of God, who gives to all liberally and
without reproach, and it will be given to
him. But let him ask in faith, with no
doubting, for he who doubts is like a wave
of the sea driven and tossed by the wind.
For let not that man suppose that he will
receive anything from the Lord; he is a
double-minded man, unstable in all his
ways."

(James 1:2-8)

In as much as we profess to be Christians, there will come a time that the challenges we face will reveal the true strength of our faith.

We might claim to want to rid doubts from our lives, but the truth is that many of us are not willing to do the will of God. It is essential to rid our minds of any negative thoughts and retract from every shell of unbelief which in effect may fight against the will of God.

One member of my church said to me *"Pastor, I believe in Jesus, but I don't believe miracles still exist."* This perception is common in the minds of many Christians who attend church every Sunday. Their minds have been clouded with doubts and they now struggle to believe in the work of the Holy Spirit. They believe that miracles are just a fantasy that existed in the 'Biblical times' and that it is not possible anymore.

However, there is one piece of evidence that still proves that the concept of miracles is still with us today – it is a miracle that many people around the world get to experience. What better miracle can be compared with getting saved and starting a new life in Christ? Is it not true that our faith gets weakened by the problems we face every day, and it can make us doubt what God can do and is already doing for us? We already picture what we want God to do for us, so our minds miss all the other blessings we have received from Him as a result of our faith. We begin to doubt God's ability to fix our situation and do not see the things He is doing for us daily. This shows the type of foundation we have built on Jesus Christ. We can express how much we love and believe in Jesus in our comfortable and pleasant moments. We talk and boast about our prayer life and how strong we are in the Lord but when a problem arises and everything seems to point to the end, the true extent of our faith and strength as Christians is revealed.

Not everyone has had that opportunity to experience the presence of God at Bethany even though some have heard about Jesus' miracles. But Jesus had a group of believers who followed him and sat under His feet. They represented the church or a house group in that small town of Bethany. But on that fateful day the death of one member named Lazarus brought the faith of this small group into question.

In order for Jesus to bring Lazarus to life, He had

to first rescue his sisters from their doubts. Martha and Mary had lost their brother, but I believe that they had also lost their confidence in what Jesus Christ could do when someone had died:

> *"Martha said to Him, 'I know that he will rise again in the resurrection at the last day.'"*
>
> *(John 11:24-26)*

A miracle at this time did not seem possible to them. I believe the two sisters were emotionally distraught with anxiety and grief. Lazarus' death may have consumed their whole mind such that they might have forgotten Jesus' true power and what He was capable of.

We can notice from this context that Martha is thinking about the last day forgetting that miracles can happen in the present. Jesus said to her:

> *"I am the resurrection and the life. He who believes in Me, though he may die, he shall*

live. And whoever lives and believes in Me
shall never die. Do you believe this?"

(John 11:25-26)

Normally we try equating our own ability to that one of God. We believe that if it is impossible for us, nobody else will be able to do it, not even God. We forget, however, that God's greatness cannot be measured, and it is infinite. The Apostle Paul says:

"... the foolishness of God is wiser than men;
and the weakness of God is stronger than
men."

(1 Corinthians 1:25)

This should, more than anything else, encourage us to ask God for help and have no doubts within us, because when we have surpassed our limit in strength, God is just getting started.

If You Would Only Believe

A person who does not believe in anything rarely receives anything. Jesus called Martha and Mary to attention when He saw they had been consumed by unbelief. We read in Matthew:

"... and he did not many mighty works there because of their unbelief."

We can now understand why Jesus told Martha and Mary to believe. In other words 'you must trust and have faith in me'.

Miracles are rare, especially when the atmosphere is full of sceptics. They do not believe in change and can only see the negative in everything. Undoubtedly one notices the pessimism in the way they talk and their deeds. They are obstacles to miracles and breakthroughs. We saw that in Jairus's house:

"When Jesus came into the ruler's house, and saw the flute players and the noisy crowd wailing, He said to them, 'Make room, for the girl is not dead, but sleeping.' And they ridiculed Him. But when the crowd was put outside, He went in and took her by

the hand, and the girl arose."

(Matthew 9:23-25)

This young girl's episode bears similarities to that of Lazarus. We all see death as the end of both stories because it appears that Jesus was late. We easily give up when our expectations are not met within our own time frame. Normally we become so worried and develop a doubtful mindset against God's plans for us.

No wonder the mourners made a mockery of Jesus' statement. Nevertheless, we as Christians must never forget that with God all things are possible. These mourners did not see the need of Jesus coming to see this young girl and therefore questioned his statement that she was asleep. No wonder Jesus asked them to leave the room before bringing her back to life.

Usually we want to see things done our way before we believe it. This kind of behaviour has led a lot of believers to seal off every opportunity they may have received from God and therefore led to costly missed opportunities. A doubtful mind and our unbelief are often the obstacles that hinder our breakthrough. It can act as the venom that seeps into our faith and completely destroys it.

There are fundamental things we need to know if we want to solely depend on God for our miracles. These things have the power to potentially dominate our way of thinking, blinding us from the path God intended for us to walk through.

Trust

When we begin to lose trust, we are immediately struck with an overwhelming sense of fear, continuously asking the same questions.

- Is there anyone who I can speak to about this?
- Who can I trust?
- Can I trust this person?

These questions can cause a constant spiral in our minds consuming our thoughts and making us contemplate whether anyone can truly be trusted.

Faith

We start to lack faith when we doubt God and His true power. This is frequently seen when things do not go as initially expected, a sharp decrease in our faith levels can come as a result of depression, bereavement, sickness, danger, and the like.

Hope

Certain situations may cause us to lose all sense of hope and security, allowing our hearts to be overthrown overcome by despair and grief. Inside of us may be a strong build-up of emotions from the dominion despair has gained over our lives and comfort becomes a distant memory as our search for hope ends in failure.

An alternative outcome may come when we ask something from God. Because it is different to our expectation, it prolongs the agony of waiting for the expected result.

Dealing With All Possible Barriers

Let us make every effort as Christians to deal with any barrier that stands between us and God. The problem we have as Christians is that we want everything to be done in an easy way; we are not willing to fight, but still expect to win. What we should remember, however, is that without the tests, we cannot succeed.

A group of friends wanted to get their paralytic friend to Jesus but realised that all access to Him was blocked. They devised a plan. They uncovered the roof and what they did paid off:

"Then they came to Him, bringing a paralytic who was carried by four men. And when they could not come near Him because of the crowd, they uncovered the roof where He was. So when they had broken through, they let down the bed on which the paralytic was lying."

(Mark 2:3-4)

Look at the faith exhibited by these men. They

knew that the only way to get their friend healed was to get him to Jesus. This was similar to the stone that covered Lazarus' tomb as Jesus knew that the only way to raise Lazarus, was to remove the stone. In both stories there were hindrances that stopped them from reaching their aim. The only difference was that when Jesus wanted the stone to be taken away, He wanted to reach the dead to give life. On the other hand, when the men removed the roof, they wanted to reach Jesus so that He could heal their friend. The fundamental issue here is that Jesus wants to reach the world and give us life as He stated in John's Gospel

> " ... I have come that they may have life,
> and that they may have it more
> abundantly."
>
> *(John 10:10b)*

However, for this to happen, we must first obey His commands by removing every hindrance from our way.

When a master speaks, it is the duty of the servants to listen to him. It is a sign of obedience and full commitment. Jesus had spoken, and so the stone had to be removed. When problems arise, do we listen to those who have the answers, or do we go by our own judgement? Now the responsibility had been passed on to two the sisters. They had to remove the stone. All of us have something that we must remove. We can never witness a miracle without participation. Apparently, Jesus had not said anything about bringing Lazarus back to life. That would have sped up the process. Humanly speaking, Lazarus was dead. Logically, he had been buried for four days. In Jewish custom four days were enough to accept that someone was legally dead. In fact, the question to remove the stone raised some doubts among the sisters. Being familiar with Jesus' healing power, they were in doubt about what He could do at this time to bring their brother back to life. In most cases, we get carried away by familiarity. As the saying goes 'familiarity breeds contempt'. Let us look at the way Jesus was received into His own hometown:

> "'Is this not the carpenter, the Son of Mary, and brother of James, Joses, Judas, and Simon? And are not His sisters here with us?' So they were offended at Him."
>
> (Mark 6:3)

The people thought they knew Jesus just because they knew his family and the work that he did, and so they negatively stereotyped Him and downplayed the importance of His words. But, if we know who Jesus truly is then we can break down these psychological barriers.

Chapter Four

A Stench May Arise

Do Not Write Me Off

A woman once gave a testimony about her son. He was sent to prison andshe was deeply worried about two problems that arose from her son's predicament: the shame that characterised a convicted prisoner in the community and the stigma that would await her and the entire family after he had served his jail time. She was assured that as long as her son was being held in the prison, his 'stench' would be locked up with him and she would not hear anyone talking about the bad odour that he had brought into the town.

One day, an old friend of her son, who is a born-again Christian, met the woman and asked the whereabouts of his friend. *"I didn't want to tell him where my son was"*, she said. *"I didn't want him to know the mess that he had gotten himself into."* It was greatly apparent that although the woman's son was being held in jail, the worry of what might happen when those prison doors were opened and he was released from his place of restrictions, was stopping her from seeking alternative ways of helping him. After considering how best to respond, she told him *"your friend is in prison"*. Despite this unpleasant news, the friend did not allow it to cause any major obstruction between them and he regularly visited the prison, meeting and conversing with his friend. These constant visits to the prison by this friend, who happened to be a Christian brought a change to the woman's son, causing him to effectively change his lifestyle. When talking about this young man, the woman explained:

"I wrote him off again and again, and I didn't have faith that God could use him to bring a change to my son's life and beliefs. Now my son has seen the light and his mess has become a message and a testimony to others."

"Therefore, if anyone is in Christ, he is a new creation; old things have passed away; behold, all things have become new."

(2 Corinthians 5:17)

Her son was released after two years; and when he came out, he was no longer a 'bad boy' known for his bad reputation, but a believer of Jesus Christ and an example to others. When this woman was giving her testimony, she said: *"I wanted to cover up the embarrassment he had caused to the family. But look at what the Lord has done."* Despite all that happened, Jesus did not write him off.

By This Time There Is A Stench

Most of us are surrounded by unpleasant things, which I call 'odours', that come out when we live without the Spirit of Christ. A life lived without Christ is not pleasant, it has no hope and it is dead. Paul writes:

"... at that time you were without Christ, being aliens from the commonwealth of

*Israel and strangers from the covenants of
promise, having no hope and without God
in the world."*

(Ephesians 2:12)

It is possible to feel that emptiness, when you live without Christ; glory becomes ugliness and our fame is turned to shame. This gives us a sign of what has become of us; and why our sweet aroma has changed to a pungent odour. A life trapped in this sinful world will most likely be meaningless until Jesus comes to save you.

Those without Christ have no life in Him; they are caged by the enemy and can rot at any time. As observed by Martha, Lazarus's sister:

*"Lord, by this time there is a stench, for he
has been dead four days."*

(John 11:39)

This statement is true as an odour arises from things which are rotten. Having spent four days in a tomb, the body would have most certainly reached its decomposed state. But we must let the truth of God speak and all the theories of men be proved wrong. We read:

> *"A man's heart plans his course, but the LORD determines his steps."*
>
> *(Proverbs 16:9)*

We think we have chosen the right path in our own eyes, until Jesus comes and makes all of our directions seem invalid. Martha was aware of the effects and the state of a person who had been dead for four days. Her understanding of the Jewish tradition and the nature of the human body weighed down her faith. No wonder she was too reluctant and not ready to co-operate with Jesus, only anticipating about the future resurrection and the problems tied with it. Her optimism had rapidly diminished in a very short space of time. She knew the horrible stages her brother had gone through; he became sick, he died and by now his decomposing body was beginning to smell. I believe that after all her brother had gone through, Martha just wanted

Lazarus to rest peacefully. Sometimes the difficulties a relative may go through can also affect you mentally and psychologically. The pain and suffering they have been through often remains in our memories and we may seem to be affected by it more than they are. It is as if there is a simultaneous emotional connection between us and our loved ones when something bad happens. However, we tend to allow this emotion to build up in us, and to override our faith, and diminishing our hope.

We should not, however, let our hope be diminished by our prejudice. How can we compare this situation to how we often view sinners as hopeless, to the circumstances that Mary and Martha were facing? This scene was the epitome of the duty of every Christian. We must work with the Lord to save lost souls, whose spirits are dead and bring them to life, rather than condemning and criticising them. Mary and Martha, as followers of Christ, had a duty to work with Jesus Christ the Lord to save the soul of

Lazarus. Will we ever be prepared to let our 'bad odours' be released and exposed to allow Christ to work a miracle? Or will we continually cover them up and block our chance of salvation? We pray for God's calling; and for Him to come to us in our time of need. However, when He arrives, we play down all His commands and decide not to follow His ways. We try to cover up and leave our "Lazarus" to rot, without being prepared to withstand the odour that might come out.

We should understand, however, that sometimes the bad odour is worth it if Jesus can do the miracle. Why should we have to cover up our sins when Jesus is there to forgive? Why should we make excuses when a little input can lead to your miracle? Jesus said:

> *"Did I not tell you that if you believe, you will see the glory of God?"*
>
> *(John 11:40)*

There has to be an element of trust.

God's Way Defeats Human Logic

Those who do not follow the divine direction of Jesus Christ are preventing the move of God and instead choosing to live their own way. It is difficult to advise a Christian who has already made up his mind on a matter based on facts and not faith. We draw and schedule our own plans and then ask God to complete the project. We see this in some of the prayer meetings and churches - people crying and asking God to hurry up and finish the work that they asked Him to do. God has become like an employee; we are the employer commanding Him to do everything accordingly. Whenever we take the matter into our own hands, we may not see the hand of God moving in our lives. We have many **'Do It Yourself'** (DIY) believers who do their own thing and blame God when they do not succeed. In the book of Jeremiah, it is written.

"Thus says the Lord: 'Let not the wise man glory in his wisdom, let not the mighty man

glory in his might, nor let the rich man glory in his riches; but let him who glories glory in this, that he understands and knows Me, that I am the Lord, exercising lovingkindness, judgement, and righteousness in the earth. For in these I delight,' says the Lord."

(Jeremiah 9:23-24)

Our sense of logic does not work within God's divine parameters. In other words, it is not possible for us to think outside of the concept of faith and get things done in God's way. This does not mean that human reasoning is irrelevant in these situations, but what I understand here is that our human logic does not compel God to do things; it rather hinders His performances. God wants his children to believe and trust him. It pleases Him when we remain faithful to his Word and understand that whatever He has promised, He will do.

However, we have all been diagnosed with a

common disease known as 'unbelief'. It is difficult to identify the unbelief syndrome until we come across situations that seem impossible. In essence, it is when we come to a conclusion of a matter and we see no sign of hope, that all lines of possible breakthrough are shut. We give up when our common sense tells us this is too much for anyone to handle. We display symptoms such as fear, reluctancy and worry daily, but most of us are not aware of the cure for this problem. The cure is **Faith**. It is the ability to rely on the Word of God, something a lot less common.

Instead of putting all their focus on the smell coming from the tomb, all Mary and Martha had to do was to put their focus on Jesus, believe in Him and remove the stone. Their reluctance was a sign of unbelief that had filled their thoughts to the point that they believed nothing good could come from their brother's tomb. They were only expecting the worse.

It is this same narrow-minded approach we

sometimes adopt in our lives, where we think that because of the 'odour' that may come through our confession, we will let the sleeping dogs lie, and deny or problems. Relatively, we behave like these sisters. We are more concerned about the "odour" that will come out when the stone of our trouble is removed, that it blinds us from the true joy of having our lifelong struggles resolved.

There is a common saying, that we should 'Stop worrying about what can go wrong and get excited about what can go right.' Sometimes we think we have faith until we find ourselves in a challenging situation; particularly when the need arises to make decisions that do not suit us. This is when we then start objecting to things and making excuses. Jesus had good plans that He intended to carry out and a good idea in mind, but these sisters were thinking solely about the bad odour that would come from opening the tomb. They made excuses and to some extent, they were preventing the move of God and the good intentions that He had for them.

Authenticity of Jesus' Words

In our world today, people of authority usually have the final verdict on situations. These people are highly esteemed. If a case comes before a judge, and the judge gives his or her verdict, there is no room for argument.

Jesus made it clear to his disciples:

> *"Did I not say to you that if you would believe you would see the glory of God?"*
>
> *(John 11:40)*

We can see how Jesus is stressing the value of the words He had spoken. In other words, *'ladies if you want to see God's glory you must, first of all, believe Him.'* If we truly believe something, we will value it. We treasure it in our hearts and hang on to every word of it. This affirmation voice tells us as Christians to accept the authenticity of the Word of God and put it into practice. Why do we give second thoughts on the orders given to us by our Saviour Jesus Christ? Why do we find it so difficult to put complete trust in Him who has promised He will take care of us? Is He not the one who gave up His own life and died for us, with the purpose that we would live eternally with God the Father in His kingdom? We second-guess our own decision-making and fail to truly believe in the authenticity of His words, even when God Himself has instructed us to believe them.

Jesus told Martha:

> *"Did I not say to you that if you would believe you would see the glory of God?"*
> (John 11:40)

In other words, Martha did not forget what she had been taught. I believe that both sisters believed Jesus to be a teacher, but they had forgotten what they had been taught as a result of the severity of the situation. If they truly believed what Jesus was capable of, they would have had no reason to doubt His power and make an excuse that would delay the miracle He had planned for them.

There are a few verses in the Bible that prove the

authenticity of Jesus' words:

"While he was still speaking, behold, a
bright cloud overshadowed them; and
suddenly a voice came out of the cloud,
saying, 'This is My beloved Son, in whom I
am well pleased. Hear Him!'"

(Matthew 17:5)

"His mother said to the servants, 'Whatever
He says to you, do it.'"

(John 2:5)

"But Simon answered and said to Him,
'Master, we have toiled all night and caught
nothing; nevertheless at Your word I will let
down the net.'"

(Luke 5:5)

At the very point when the fishermen were thinking of stopping, Jesus told them to cast their nets to the other side of the boat. It was their hopelessness and desperation that made them do it, even though they had told Jesus about the struggles they had had all night long.

We are God's Sweet Aroma

The Bible affirms:

> *"... we are to God the fragrance of Christ among those who are being saved and among those who are perishing."*
>
> *(2 Corinthians 2:15)*

There are many out there who don't want Jesus to know the state of their lives. Their lives seem so bad that even the mention of an improvement is a difficult topic for them to grasp. They prefer to show their pride in their outward appearance and suffer the hell within. They are very aware of the embarrassment they would feel if the pastor was to get a hint of their ugly story. These are the people who go to Church behaving like everything is 'ok', greeting people, engaging in conversation and exchanging compliments but show a slight indication somewhere that something is not right.

Our so-called 'wisdom' as humans sometimes give us the wrong judgements in some situations. We worry about the things we do not know and condemn the things we do not understand. Basically, Mary and Martha had no idea what would come after the bad odour. What we do know, is that Jesus Christ was not there to mourn the death of his friend with them; this may have caused them to doubt the loyalty of Jesus' friendship.

This was not His prime objective, however. He had a good plan for His dead friend. The Apostle Paul reminds his reader of that which Isaiah wrote:

> *"... Eye has not seen, nor ear heard, nor have entered into the heart of man, the things which God has prepared for those who love Him."*
>
> *(1 Corinthians 2:9, Isaiah 64:4)*

God's plan for us is to give us hope for our future. He longs for us to have purposeful lives, but at the same time, God does not condone our sinful acts. He will not condemn us for them, but it is true that bad odours come out from us in our sinful state. To be able to get rid of these odours, we have to change the state of death by the admittance of Jesus. The Apostle John recorded the purpose for which Jesus came:

> *"For God did not send His Son into the world to condemn the world, but that the world through Him might be saved."*
>
> *(John 3:17)*

We have to understand that things do not rot when there is life in them.

Chapter Five

Lazarus Come Forth

Open Day for a Miracle

A scene of triumph in the land of Bethany unfolded. It appeared as though death had won the contest by keeping Lazarus under its grip for four days. The hopes and expectations of the family had died with him, leaving everyone to cry and mourn with Martha and Mary. Four days away from reality, bitten by the sting of death and kept by the dominion of its power, Lazarus was in a state which caused major distress in the town of Bethany. His sickness led to death and then to the tomb.

His siblings were perplexed to witness these fateful moments in the absence of Jesus, believing that the story could have changed if He had been there. But the good news is that if the story did change in His absence, then it could also change in His presence.

The Bible records the story of the widow in Nain, who lost her son - her only son. On that fateful day as they were going to bury him, they had a surprise divine encounter. The funeral procession came to standstill, as Jesus was moved with compassion by the state of this widow:

> *"When the Lord saw her, He had compassion on her and said to her, 'Do not weep.'"*
>
> *(Luke 7:13)*

It takes someone who understands your condition to tell you not to weep at this situation. Jesus takes our pain, grief and sorrow to heart. Being heart broken and immersed in the tragedy of her son, Jesus encouraged her to weep not. He touched the coffin and commanded the young man to arise.

> *"Then He came and touched the open coffin, and those who carried him stood still, and He said, 'Young man, I say to you,*

arise.'"

(Luke 7:14)

Now the scene of mourning had become an atmosphere of praise. Everything had turned around; the widow was no longer weeping, and the young man was alive again. Now the tables have turned; a miracle had occurred at the village gate. Jesus brought an end to their weeping, asked the dead to get up and then gave him back to his mother. No one ever meets Jesus and returns the same. Those that met Him empty, returned full. Those that were blind regained their sight, and the lame began to walk.

We may have our bad days and troubled moments, but God has made every day as important as each other. Let's consider this analogy. For a plant to survive and grow to bear fruits, it must endure all seasons and weathers; the storms, the sunshine and the rain.

"In the day of prosperity be joyful, But in the day of adversity consider: Surely God

has appointed the one as well as the other,
So that man can find out nothing that will
come after him."

Irrespective of any situation, let us hold on to the Lord in prayer, and allow Him to take charge.

In fact, what God will do in the midst of our predicament will literally shock us. What could have been a loss will definitely be to our profit and what could have caused pain will turn to our gain.

This is what was described by Apostle Paul:

"Having disarmed principalities and powers,
He made a public spectacle of them,
triumphing over them in it."

(Colossians 2:15)

The shackles, the fetters and all the yokes have all come to nothing. But who has the power to invade the place of death, where invaders go and never come back? Jesus explained that:

"No one can enter a strong man's house
and plunder his goods, unless he first binds
the strong man, and then he will plunder his
house."

(Mark 3:27)

Whose voice shakes the foundation of death? Apostle John records Jesus' words:

"Do not marvel at this; for the hour is
coming in which all who are in the graves
will hear His voice."

(John 5:28)

This voice is the overwhelming voice of Christ in God: it is the voice that gives the gift of life and light, peace and serenity, restoration and strength. God's ears are always open when there is a cry from His children, He always finds a solution to allow peace and happiness to re-emerge. Just as a father hears and attends to the cry of his child, the same way the Lord hears our cries. The psalmist reflects:

"You number my wanderings; put my tears

into Your bottle; are they not in Your book?
When I cry out to You, then my enemies will
turn back; this I know, because God is for
me."

Making Prayer Our Priority

Prayer forms the basis of our connection with God and serves as a reflection of how our relationship is with Him. The Bible instructs us to *"pray without ceasing."* (1 Thessalonians 5:17) In essence we should not get tired of praying about anything whether it seems good or bad. Everything we do must start and end with prayer. When we do this, we allow God to decide on every matter and make His own conclusions afterwards. Based on the content of Jesus' prayers, I believe that before Jesus made that trip to Bethany, He had already offered prayers to His father:

"... and Jesus lifted up His eyes and said,
'Father, I thank You that You have heard
Me. And I know that You always hear Me,

*but because of the people who are standing
by I said this, that they may believe that You
sent Me."*

Before Jesus spoke to the dead man Lazarus, He gave thanks to God. It was a prayer of purpose acknowledging God for what He had already done. The Apostle Paul encourages us, using the words of Isaiah and Jesus to:

*"Be anxious for nothing, but in everything
by prayer and supplication, with
thanksgiving, let your requests be made
known to God."*

(Philippians 4:6, Isaiah 55:22 & Matthew 6:25)

We do not need to worry after casting all our problems on the Lord. We just need God's way and His order. There are many times that we have gone ahead of God with our own initiative. But let us understand that before making any decision whatsoever we should never forget to consult the Lord. Never speak about your problems before you speak to God. In all circumstances, we should let God know. We should pray and get feedback from Him before we do anything which will have serious implications for us.

Come Forth

A voice has granted our freedom, giving us the insight to realise that we are no longer slaves, but we are free. In fact, for some of us, the memories of perilous times and the fears of our past have enabled us to embark on this Christian journey without any hesitation. We have come too far to return to our mess, and compromise all the heavenly privileges that God, through His Son Jesus, gave us.

The Christian journey that we embark on has required too much dedication for us to remain dormant without any commitment, so we ought not to remain still. There is a wind of Fire blowing around us; a Holy Fire burning up of every dead work in order for the glory of the Lord to be revealed.

There is no life in the grave, no hope in the broken home, no love in a broken relationship; no chance for anything to *'come forth'*. However, Jesus defies all human logic when He says:

"... he who hears My word and believes in Him who sent Me has everlasting life, and shall not come into judgement, but has passed from death into life. Most assuredly, I say to you, the hour is coming, and now is, when the dead will hear the voice of the Son of God; and those who hear will live."

(John 5:24-25)

The Apostle Peter was wise to ask Jesus if he could come to Him on the water. He spoke to Jesus:

"... and said, 'Lord, if it be thou, bid me come unto thee on the water' and He said, 'Come' and when Peter was come down out of the ship, he walked on the water, to go to Jesus"

(Matthew 14:28-29 KJV)

He knew the consequences of trying something

without Jesus' approval. If he did not ask Jesus, he could have drowned. We must ask God if what we are doing is the right thing to do before we try, otherwise, it could end badly.

When we overcome the trouble of our past, and it no longer has any power over us. The prophet Isaiah records God's promise:

"I will say to the prisoners, 'Come out in freedom,' and to those in darkness, 'Come into the light.' They will be my sheep, grazing in green pastures and on hills that were previously bare."

(Isaiah 49:9)

Jesus took that which was insignificant; He called out for the glory stuck in our past and made it relevant for our present. Maybe the story of your past has kept you worried and those that know you have slammed the door in your face. You have a choice either to continue to remain captive and live in darkness or come out and enjoy the light of His presence.

We can be far from the presence of God but that can never keep us away from hearing His voice. God has made His plea that we should all come to Him, from the young children struggling through childhood to the adults who suffer adversity day after day. In fact, it does not matter the state of our sin and how far we have left His presence, He has made open an invitation for us to come now to Him. Remember God's promise:

> *"'Come now, and let us reason together,'*
> *says the Lord, 'though your sins are like*
> *scarlet, they shall be as white as snow;*
> *though they are red like crimson, they shall*
> *be as wool.'"*
>
> *(Isaiah 1:18)*

Honouring this invitation will bring an end to the shame we have acquired through sin. We can see in the verse above how God is ready to make our lives as white as snow:

> *"... He said to them, 'Those who are well*
> *have no need of a physician, but those who*

are sick. I did not come to call the righteous,
but sinners, to repentance.'"

(Mark 2:17)

Just as Jesus called Lazarus, likewise He is calling for all of those that are dead in sin to have life and live again.

At the town of Bethany, there was a showcase when the stone was removed for Lazarus to come forth. All focus was on the entrance of the tomb; to the amazement of all those watching, Lazarus's body came forth wrapped in grave cloth. Now the womb of the grave had opened for Lazarus to be a sign and a testament of the power of God. A sign of spiritual awakening became a symbol of testimony in the town of Bethany to show that it is not only the living that can hear the voice of God. Even though he was dead, Lazarus was able to hear the voice of Jesus calling to him, thereby confirming His resurrection power. It is so powerful it can communicate with the dead. We recall the words of Jesus:

"Do not marvel at this; for the hour is coming in which all who are in the graves will hear His voice and come forth - those who have done good, to the resurrection of life, and those who have done evil, to the resurrection of condemnation."

(John 5:28-29)

Reasons We Should Respond To God's Call To Come Forth

Come If You Need Parental Affection

"Therefore 'Come out from among them and be separate', says the Lord. 'Do not touch what is unclean, and I will receive you. I will be a Father to you, and you shall be My sons and daughters', says the Lord Almighty."

(2 Corinthians 6:17-18)

Come If You Are Thirsty

Jesus is calling those who are thirsty to come and

enjoy living water:

*"... and the Spirit and the bride say, 'Come!'
and let him who hears say, 'Come!' and let
him who thirsts come. Whoever desires, let
him take the water of life freely."*

(Revelation 22:17)

If we really know the one beckoning us, we will
not make any excuses.

Come If You Are In Need

*"Ho! Everyone who thirsts, come to the
waters; and you who have no money, come,
buy and eat. Yes, come, buy wine and milk
without money and without price"*

(Isaiah 55:1)

We are assured that those who come to Him will
not lack any good thing, and whether it is be our
spiritual or physical need, it will be catered for.

Come If You Are Weary

"Come to Me, all you who labour and are

heavy laden, and I will give you rest."

Jesus has given us an open invitation to come to His place of rest. To recall the reasons for the nervousness and dissatisfaction present in humanity, we may ask ourselves how we can cope with the burdens of life.

It is Time to Leave the Tomb

What would you do if you were put in the situation where you had to make a choice to follow orders and be free, or be defiant and remain bound? Would you respond and come forth or would you ignore it? Those who have committed a criminal offence and have been restrained by the law, must do what the law requires. However, when the law is revoked, they are at liberty to walk free without any further restrictions.

Having been a 'lonely tenant' in the grave for some days, Lazarus was clealry dead. But death could not hold him captive, neither did it prevent him from responding to the loud voice of our Lord Jesus Christ when He called Lazarus' name.

Our gaining freedom from the situations which hold us captive, may depend on the total obedience to the voice of the Lord Jesus Christ:

> *"... He designates a certain day, saying in David, 'Today' after such a long time, as it has been said: 'Today, if you will hear His voice, do not harden your hearts.'"*
>
> *(Hebrews 4:7, Psalm 95:7)*

There is a saying that *'procrastination is a thief of time'*. We should not wait for another opportunity because it may be that we will be too late, or we shall never get another one. There were so many people Jesus could have brought to life, but he chose to call *you*. Like Lazarus, Jesus will specifically call your name.

In fact, the dead man came out alive without any hesitation. He did not say *"I can't see you"* nor *"I can't walk"*; he just responded by following the voice. When we respond to His call, we shall surely leave the world behind us. Lazarus came out from the grave as life entered him. I believe Martha and Mary were surprised to see their brother Lazarus emerge without the expected rotting body and smell.

Jesus has Power over Death

Even death is no match for the supernatural power of God. He stripped away the power of death:

> *"O Death, where is your sting? O Hades,*
> *where is your victory?"*
>
> *(1 Corinthians 15:55 from Hosea 13:14)*

We are not, in any way, able to comprehend the miracles He does for us daily. From the outermost and to the innermost regions of the world, nothing can restrain or match the manifestation of God's power.

His power is awesome, and it is evidenced by the following scriptures:

> *"The Lord kills and makes alive; He brings*

down to the grave and brings up."

(1 Samuel 2:6)

Let us take a look at the following Bible verses and see the overwhelming power God has over death:

"He will swallow up death forever, and the Lord God will wipe away tears from all faces; The rebuke of His people He will take away from all the earth; for the Lord has spoken."

(Isaiah 25:8)

"But God will redeem my soul from the power of the grave, for He shall receive me."

(Psalm 49:15)

"Your dead shall live; Together with my dead body, they shall arise. Awake and sing, you who dwell in dust; For your dew is like the dew of herbs, And the earth shall cast out the dead."

(Isaiah 26:19)

"... but has now been revealed by the appearing of our Saviour Jesus Christ, who has abolished death and brought life and immortality to light through the gospel."

(2 Timothy 1:10)

There are many circumstances in the Bible where God restored life to people. You many be aware of the vision God showed to Ezekiel to prophesy life over the dry bones piled up in the valley. (Ezekiel 37)

Prophet Ezekiel saw no hope for life in the dry bones. They had passed the stage of identification and for that matter could not be recognised.

In your 'dry bone' moments, you may recall the thing that once lived but now is dead; once good, but now bad, once beautiful, but now ugly. You cannot predict the outcomes because to all intents and purposes, they are beyond repair.

The power of death may have sunk all hope, leaving us with more questions than answers. In Ezekiel's account of The Valley of Dry Bones, God inquired of him:

"'Son of man, can these bones live?' So I answered, 'O Lord God, You know.'"

Similarly, God can ask you if there is a way forward in your situation. Clearly he had no clue as to how a miracle could come out of it. As a matter of fact, no-one could expect a miracle in this kind of situation. I know we Christians believe in miracles. We may have heard of the dead coming back to life again, the blind and dumb receiving miraculous healing during crusades. But if you ask me to pray for a 'dry bone' to come back to life, doubt will overwhelm me.

By the grace of God, Lazarus' journey to the grave turned out to be a mere visit. God's grace found him, and he walked out and re-entered the land of the living. Actually, the grace of God opens doors for our freedom and rescues us from all manner of trouble. We have the assurance that:

"... the grace of God that brings salvation

has appeared to all men."

(Titus 2:11)

This is a life-changing watchword, and the redemption power of God is available to all. It has been revealed through our Lord Jesus Christ. Let us look at Lazarus's case - his final destination was certified but it was revoked by grace. He heard and responded to a higher calling from the Lord, and he was freed from the shackles of death. He was called out of darkness to the light, from an awful place to the awesome presence of the living God.

Grace Found us and Changed our Place

See how God can alter our ugly moments for the manifestation of His glory. The psalmist expressed his amazement as follows:

"When the Lord brought back the captivity
of Zion, we were like those who dream.
Then our mouth was filled with laughter,
and our tongue with singing. Then they said
among the nations, 'The Lord has done

great things for them.' The Lord has done
great things for us, and we are glad."

(Psalm 126:1-3)

This was a glorious homecoming for Lazarus because Jesus needed him and therefore gave him a new birth. Lazarus's death shows how helpless human beings can be without the Lord. It previews our hopeless state in this fallen world. How can we be playing and laughing in one moment and then suddenly, without warning, we are gone and become history in a matter of moments?

Today, we might be able to go to the gym and train, working tirelessly just to get our bodies fit and healthy, but a time will come when we can hardly lift ourselves up without someone's help. The voice of your children, your spouse and other loved ones will no longer get your attention.

A baby born into this world can bring happiness and joy to a family, but their departure can cause a mixture of sorrow and grief. We are warned of the unavoidable reality:

"To everything there is a season, a time for every purpose under heaven; a time to be born, and a time to die ..."

Our existence on earth is for a season during which time we must serve its purpose. It is essential to find out how we can serve and worship the Lord to the uttermost, as this is our reasonable service on earth:

"Lord, make me to know my end, and what is the measure of my days, that I may know how frail I am."

(Psalm 39:4)

One of the most important things as Christians is to be alive in the Spirit and dead to self.

Let us shift our attention to the book Genesis when Adam was forewarned of the curse which would result from disobedience *"... for in the day that you eat of it you shall surely die."* (Genesis 2:17)

Spiritually, Adam died in the sight of God. Even though he lived, he could not serve the Lord. He was physically alive and spiritually dead, and we should remember that we do not worship the Lord with our flesh:

> "So then, those who are in the flesh cannot please God."
>
> *(Romans 8:8)*

The reality is they were spiritually unconscious and alienated from the presence of the living God. Now before we can get back into His presence, God must call us again:

> "... who has saved us and called us with a holy calling, not according to our works, but according to His own purpose and grace which was given to us in Christ Jesus before time began, but has now been revealed by the appearing of our Saviour Jesus Christ, who has abolished death and brought life and immortality to light through the

gospel."

(2 Timothy 1:9-10)

Like Lazarus, we cannot save ourselves and nobody can do that for us except God. But thanks be to God who has brought our salvation, through Jesus Christ who has overcome death once and for all.

Chapter Six

The Glory of the latter day

Free At Last

It is within God's redemption plan that we experience freedom from both spiritual and physical bondage. We all long for the most complete freedom because if we look at the alternative - slavery and bondage - we know exactly where we want to be. The problem is an increasing wave of fear coming from those who were once oppressed. They ignorantly allow themselves to suffer from the nightmares of their past. Jesus has granted us our freedom from the enemy's oppression and so we are obliged to walk as children of the Most High and not as slaves any longer. Our freedom is authored and guaranteed by the work on the Cross of Calvary.

As a matter of fact, no person in a position of power nor any 'spiritual being' can alter our liberty as Christians. The Apostle Paul reminds us:

"For you, brethren, have been called to liberty; only do not use liberty as an opportunity for the flesh ..."

(Galatians 5:13)

Let us not forget where we were before we became Christians - being controlled by the desires of the flesh and suffering at the hands of our enemies. We had no choice but to suffer the punishment for our iniquities, but we were pardoned by the grace of our Lord Jesus Christ. We were condemned by the law to face the charges due it, but the precious blood of Jesus spoke on our behalf. Knowing this freedom as believers, we should live in accordance with the measure of grace given to us if we want to avoid any evil traps. It is not acceptable to walk as slaves when we have been promised to walk as kings. The Bible states:

"If the Son therefore shall make you free, you shall be free indeed." (John 8:36) Therefore, let us be more conscious of ourselves and walk in the

freedom which Christ gave us, and stop holding on to the shackles and the fetters that had once kept us away from our love for the Lord.

I remember and cherish the moment that I was saved. I have never in my life felt that amount of peace that came to rest in my heart. The people that knew me, who were already believers, were happy when they saw me attending church and Christian youth programmes. Some thought it was a joke, but others were glad to believe that God had answered their prayers. It all happened one night, around 2 a.m., when I heard a voice calling my name. The voice was so loud that I immediately woke up from my sleep thinking that my brother was calling me, and all of a sudden, I started seeing flashbacks of my life. How fortunate that my life was saved by the help of God. Tears welled up in my eyes and I felt inside me a unique joy after the encounter - one that I have never experienced before. I woke my brother up and explained what had happened to him, and how God wanted to be in control of my whole life. That night, I made a decision and I gave my life to Jesus Christ. It meant that from that moment on, I had to forsake my previous lifestyle. In fact, letting go of old habits was a bit of a struggle for me, as I was hooked up with certain things which I found difficult to get rid of.

But one week after my confession, God led a Man of God into my life. He taught me how I should pray and how to allow the Holy Spirit to have His way in me. The Pastor saw my problems and he helped me to disentangle myself from my old lifestyle and stand firm in the Lord. Indeed, Christians are encouraged to:

> *"Stand fast therefore in the liberty by which Christ has made us free, and do not be entangled again with a yoke of bondage."*
>
> *(Galatians 5:1)*

In his second letter, Peter spells it out clearly:

> *"For if, after they have escaped the pollutions of the world through the knowledge of the LORD and Saviour Jesus*

Christ, they are again entangled in them and overcome, the latter end is worse for them than the beginning. For it would have been better for them not to have known the way of righteousness, than having known it, to turn from the holy commandment delivered to them. But it has happened to them according to the true proverb: 'A dog returns to his own vomit,' and, 'a sow, having washed, to her wallowing in the mire.'"

(2 Peter 2:20-22)

Since unclean things can be a distraction, we should be aware that whatever obstructs our faith, can also destroy our relationship with Him who saved us.

Loose Him

Lazarus came forth - released to unleash his God-given potential. He was a living testament to the resurrection power of God and testimony that, against all odds, God's perfect plans for people will certainly come to pass. But it was very clear that Lazarus was not free; he still had his grave clothes on. These clothes had served their purpose during his time of death and now that Lazarus had risen, they would be a hindrance. It is necessary that we avoid or leave behind any ungodly habits or characteristics. It would be counterproductive to wash, and then put your dirty clothes back on. In other words, it is wrong to be saved and still pursue your old lifestyle.

According to the Apostle Paul:

> *"You were taught, with regard to your former way of life, to put off your old self, which is being corrupted by its deceitful desires; to be made new in the attitude of your minds; and to put on the new self, created to be like God in true righteousness and holiness"*
>
> *(Ephesians 4:22-24 NIV)*

But the unfortunate thing is that we still hang onto the same habits and character after being saved. Because of this, every move to press forward seems to be a struggle.

The writer of Hebrews encourages us:

> *"Therefore we also, since we are surrounded by so great a cloud of witnesses, let us lay aside every weight, and the sin which so easily ensnares us, and let us run with endurance the race that is set before us, looking unto Jesus, the author and finisher of our faith, who for the joy that was set before Him endured the cross, despising the shame, and has sat down at the right hand of the throne of God"*
>
> *(Hebrews 12:1-2)*

If we don't leave our sinful tendencies behind in the grave, there will be no evidence that we have emerged from the old life.

Jesus did not come out of the tomb with His grave clothes. He left them in the grave (as evidence) to prove that He had risen from the dead. When the Apostle John arrived at the tomb:

"... he bent over and looked in at the strips of linen lying there but did not go in. Then Simon Peter came along behind him and went straight into the tomb. He saw the strips of linen lying there, as well as the cloth that had been wrapped around Jesus' head. The cloth was still lying in its place, separate from the linen"

(John 20:5-7 NIV)

Jesus' reaction when Lazarus came out was *"Loose Him"* (John 11:44) Jesus gave the command because it is possible to have life but still be limited in your progress. Moreover until you are totally loosed, you remain partially bound. Those who want to follow Jesus Christ are sometimes unable to do so because they are bound in the grave clothes of tradition, addiction and certain vices. If indeed you are wrapped up and bound by religious traditions, your freedom is at stake until you are physically and spiritually liberated.

Untie Me, I Want To Serve The Lord

One day Jesus was coming into Jerusalem and needed means of coming into the city. He sent his disciples to untie a colt from the city and bring it to Him to ride on. It is recorded that:

"... He said to them, 'Go into the village opposite you; and as soon as you have entered it you will find a colt tied, on which no one has sat. Loose it and bring it.'"

(Mark 11:2)

The donkey will not have known that it had been chosen for this purpose. It had been tied up, waiting for its owner to take it to the next place, and was completely unaware of the importance it would serve for the Lord. It was a favourable day for the donkey. There were so many donkeys tied up in different places, but that was the one that Jesus specifically requested.

There is always an opportunity for us to be called at an unexpected time. We will be stationary, waiting to make our next move at one point, and then called by the Lord at the right time to fulfil our purpose. God knows the areas in our lives where we are not being fruitful and useful. Many lives, however, are handicapped and ruined by an unfulfilled and unfruitful lifestyle.

Jesus called Lazarus at this time to fulfil his life and bring forth fruit. Lazarus was called forth from death and became alive once again. Whilst no longer dead, he was still bound physically, and so was unable to move effectively. He needed help, and even though he had come back to life, there was still work to be done because of grave clothes. It masked his identity and it needed to be taken off. This caused major obstruction and restriction to his movements.

Clearly, Lazarus was saved but he had issues that held him bound. The joy of seeing him come out of the tomb would not be complete until his hands, feet and face were free from the bondage. He was supposed to be free from problems yet had certain issues to deal with. He was out of the grave but not its clothes. He would have to live his life above any kind of stigma that awaited his homecoming.

When a gentleman was released from prison with a tag on his leg, his friend asked him what was on his leg. He said *"... even though I am out, I am not totally free. My movements are restricted and there are some places I cannot go. I will be free when they remove it."* The tag distinctively tells his community a story of his current identity. It is a story that links him to a particular kind of issue that is associated with the tag. That small tag reminds him of where he was and where he cannot go. But the very moment they remove it, he will be free to go anywhere he wants.

We were all dead, having our sinful clothes on, until Jesus died and set us free. He set us free so that we might have life. In essence, it is not until our sinful tag is removed, that we are free from our prison sentences.

Many people are not comfortable with their lives

because they are wearing something that raises a lot of questions. They have burdens that have not been taken notice of by the church and matters that need to be solved. Some of these people are in our churches struggling with issues but their problems are not the concern of our modern-day religious leaders. They have burdens that have not been dealt with through prayer. The voice of Jesus is still echoing to this day, *"untie and let him go"*.

We see many Christians who are still where they are because they are hooked and overpowered by sin. Blessed are those who will see your problem and remember you in their prayers, who will untie you from your past and not criticise you. Imagine if Lazarus had had no one to untie him. It is important for us as Christians to look after one another as we are one another's keepers.

Take Off Your Grave Clothes

Why do we have to live our lives as if nothing has happened inside us? It is about time we took off our grave clothes and lived right. Our new life should be reflective of the change that is associated with it. Let us understand that those clothes belong to the grave - we cannot and should not live with them once we have left the tomb. Our redemption has brought us new life and victory, so we do not need any reminder of dead things showing us our past and the shame from our past. Let us take a closer look at ourselves and see what kind of garments we have on.

We should not just focus on this great transition without emphasis on sanctification which leads to the righteousness of God, and this transition must be a continuous process until the coming of the Lord. We must understand that to get a piece of pure gold, all the dross must be removed from it. A perfect piece of gold is the one refined through fire.

What is this sanctification you ask? It is a progressive change through the perfect work of

God:

> *"Now may the God of peace Himself sanctify you completely; and may your whole spirit, soul, and body be preserved blameless at the coming of our LORD Jesus Christ. He who calls you is faithful, who also will do it."*
>
> *(1 Thessalonians 5:23-24)*

It is through the mercy and grace of our Lord Jesus Christ that our sins are pardoned by the work that was carried out on the cross. We should be mindful of our character and conduct so that we don't undermine the grace and mercies offered to us by God, or else we will open doors for the enemy to accuse us. The change that has happened inside us, will literally affect our outside.

Even the devil knows God's standard of righteousness, and so he made an accusation against the High Priest, Joshua. (Zechariah 3)

One day Joshua was accused by Satan, but Satan

was rebuked by the Lord. The Lord ordered that Joshua's filthy garments be removed; these filthy garments were a reproach for Joshua. (Zechariah 3:1-5)

It is no different for us - filthy garments give the enemy a platform to remind us of our deeds. It enables him to bombard us with fear through his false accusations. This is not the life God wants us to live - He wants us to remove these garments and live a life of freedom.

> *"Then he showed me Joshua the High Priest standing before the Angel of the LORD, and Satan standing at his right hand to oppose him, and the LORD said to Satan, 'The LORD rebuke you, Satan! The LORD who has chosen Jerusalem rebuke you! Is this not a brand plucked from the fire?' Now Joshua was clothed with filthy garments, and was standing before the Angel. Then He answered and spoke to those who stood before Him, saying, 'Take away the filthy*

garments from him,' and to him He said,
'See, I have removed your iniquity from you,
and I will clothe you with rich robes,' and I
said, 'Let them put a clean turban on his
head.' So they put a clean turban on his
head, and they put the clothes on him, and
the Angel of the LORD stood by."

(Zechariah 3:1-5, NKJV)

The garments which cover us are important when we stand in the presence of God. We are to wear clean garments without any stain when we appear before the Almighty God, holy and righteous as He is. The Apostle Paul encouraged Christians to:

"... clothe yourself with the presence of the
Lord Jesus Christ. And don't let yourself
think about ways to indulge your evil
desires."

(Romans 13:14, NLT)

We should also have character codes for our walk with the Lord. These should be our codes of conduct which lead us to the right path. It puzzles me why dress codes seem to be so important at certain events. They are purposely put in place to allow a sense of harmony and unity among members of the group. In some places, you are not even allowed through the front door without the appropriate attire or costume, which shows the importance clothes have in various situations!

Lazarus, at the time that he came out of the grave, was wrapped in grave clothes; this clothing was appropriate considering where he had just been. But the question is - was it relevant to where he was going? Grave clothes are not suitable to wear in the 'Land of the Living'. Your place and identity have changed so there is a need for you to discard your grave clothes to announce yourself as one saved from death.

Someone who has been released from prison will not continue to wear their prison clothes, not even on parole. They will be glad that they have been freed from behind bars, and so will get rid of anything that serves as a reminder of the place where they once were.

When The Lord Steps Into Our Troubled World

We See Repentance And New Life

Repentance begins when we become 'God-centred' and not 'Self-centred'. When we take away our 'Self-centred' nature and focus on God, this is when we begin to thrive in our new lives.

In order for Lazarus to start to flourish in his new life in the way that Jesus intended, he had to be totally and entirely free from any ties to his previous life.

A growing plant will not hold on to its old petals and leaves; it will instead let these go and blossom into the flower it was meant to become.

We all wish to see a generation where our society is upright with good moral standards. It is part of the world's quest to see our communities witness a revolution of kindness, and for all of us to develop a good character. Very often, people want to see a change, but they are not ready to embrace a new life in the Lord. They want to see the light, but they are not ready to come out from the darkness. Lazarus was about to rot in the grave until he came out. If we so choose, we can all be adamant in rejecting God's rescue plan for our salvation.

He Will Give You Joy For Your Sorrow

In the town of Bethany, the atmosphere of weeping and sorrow had turned to celebration and jubilation because of Jesus' arrival. In fact, God is able to transform any feeling of mourning into a time happiness, as seen in Jeremiah:

> *"Then shall the virgin rejoice in the dance,*
> *and the young men and the old, together;*
> *for I will turn their mourning to joy, will*
> *comfort them, and make them rejoice*
> *rather than sorrow."*

(Jeremiah 31:13)

Our moment of pain and grief won't stay with us forever because there are prophetic dates and seasons where things will turn for our good as the Lord takes His rightful place in our lives.

"I say to you that likewise there will be more joy in heaven over one sinner who repents than over ninety-nine just persons who need no repentance."

(Luke 15:7)

In as much as we rejoice when someone repents from any kind of sin, heaven does more-so.

He Makes All Things Beautiful

Whenever we call on God and allow Him to step into our situation, we see His glory at the end. Sometimes it may seem like everything is working against us.

The enemy will begin to whisper to you, *"Where is your God?"* You may even end up in a situation thinking no help is coming to you from anywhere. But always remember to remain faithful as His promises are true. We may experience delays sometimes and even suffer at the beginning, but the good news is that all things will point to His divine and perfect will.

Look at Joseph - where was God at the beginning of his predicament? God revealed to him in a dream what he would be. But his life didn't start out that way. However, through it all and against all odds, the perfect will of God concerning his life was fulfilled. Everything was going contrary to the dream he had but, in the end, the cloth of shame was removed from him. He came out of the prison and he became a prominent figure in Egypt:

> *"Then Pharaoh took his signet ring off his hand and put it on Joseph's hand, and he clothed him in garments of fine linen and put a gold chain around his neck."*
>
> *(Genesis 41:42)*

In the end, Joseph's story brought glory to the Lord even though he had no idea what God's vision meant concerning his life. God changed his prison place, changed his clothes and changed his position.

For Our Salvation

Lazarus could not have saved himself from the grave since there is no such thing as 'self-salvation'.

> *"Therefore He is also able to save to the uttermost those who come to God through Him, since He always lives to make intercession for them."*
>
> *(Hebrews 7:25)*

Those who are in the darkness and have lived their whole life in this place, don't know anything other than darkness. Humanity seems to find themselves stuck in this state until Jesus enters. He came as the Light and Redeemer. Jesus authored the total freedom for Lazarus as he was unable to do so by himself. Lazarus needed someone to demand on his behalf that he should be set free. Like Lazarus sinners cannot save themselves. They are helpless by themselves. Sinners must hear a voice to give them a sense of direction. We are all like lost sheep following the voice of the shepherd.

> *"I have come as a light into the world, that whoever believes in Me should not abide in darkness."*
>
> *(John 12:46)*

Let Him Go

Lazarus was called out; he was loosed and now was set free to go on with his life. When all hindrances are out of the way and the journey is all planned out, we should not waste time; but we must proceed to fulfil our God-given dream.

We all have been redeemed, justified, sanctified to *"Go Out"* to the world and tell the world about what the Lord has done for us and carry out the Great Commission. In Mark's gospel, we are told:

> *"Go into all the world and preach the gospel*

to every creature."

(Mark 16:15)

The world needs to hear the Good News, but it won't happen unless we go out and preach it. When the Apostles were arrested and put in jail, they were set free by the Angel of the Lord and they were asked to *"Go"* and give the people the message of life:

> *"But at night an angel of the Lord opened the prison doors and brought them out, and said, Go, stand in the temple and speak to the people all the words of this life."*

(Acts 5:19-20)

God does not want the disciples to be kept in jail when the people in the temple lack the message of life.

Despite Lazarus's release, a grasping hand from the grave was still keeping him attached to the dead things he had been previously associated with. He was not called from the grave to be allowed to suffer in other areas in his life; Jesus made sure that Lazarus was completely free. Proverbs informs us:

> "When you walk, your steps will not be hindered, and when you run, you will not stumble."
>
> (Proverbs 4:12)

Since we have been set free to carry out the journey in the path of righteousness, we must make sure that we do everything humanly possible and do away with anything that could restrain our self-confidence in the Lord. The danger we have in our Christian life is when we find ourselves continually fastening the knot of the 'dead' things in our lives that cause us to be tied up and deprive us of the freedom that had been given to us before. It acts as a constant connection to our problems and therefore limits our ability to maximise our potential in God.

There are so many examples of 'Lazarus' in our modern-day society. He symbolises those who are saved from seemingly impossible situations but are still deprived of certain attributes that we would associate with those who are regarded as free. Such people can be considered as being spiritually dead and are in desperate need of a resurrection. Something must be removed from their lives to prevent them from continuing their walk in darkness, and from flipping through the pages of their history one by one and gradually becoming more and more engrossed in it until they find that there is no way (or so it appears) for them to be set free. In reality, they have responded to the calling of God in their lives but do not have enough control over their bodies to co-operate with Him.

When our actions are impaired and entangled by satanic intervention, fervent prayer is needed. As Christians, we are guaranteed a full measure of liberty created by our Lord Jesus. It is not until we are mentally and physically freed, that we can walk in this freedom without restrictions. Therefore, let us not live and behave like slaves by submitting ourselves to our captors. The Apostle

Paul encouraged us to:

"Stand fast therefore in the liberty by which
Christ has made us free, and do not be
entangled again with a yoke of bondage."

(Galatians 5:1)

Lazarus was still entangled in his grave clothes of bondage when Jesus called him out. This is why Jesus gave the command for the family to loose him. It is sad when those who are close to us cannot see our pains and struggles. Lazarus was out but remained trapped in the grave clothes. Once he was dead and trapped in the tomb, but now he was alive, with grave clothes still stuck on his body.

As mentioned before it is the same as coming out of prison with your chains and prison clothes still on. Normally those who have finished their prison sentences do not come out with their prison clothes; they cannot continue to wear these clothes when they have finished their prison sentence. There would be a problem with adapting to society, and a question would be asked about the validity of their freedom.

God will never leave any stone unturned when He is dealing with our situations. He has certified our freedom so nothing should be a hindrance and He wants us to break free from all the problems that have encompassed us, and go and testify about His goodness. This mandate is clear from Peter's affirmation:

> *"But you are a chosen generation, a royal priesthood, a holy nation, His own special people, that you may proclaim the praises of Him who called you out of darkness into His marvellous light."*

(1 Peter 2:9)

Maybe right now everything may look dark. You may not see and understand what is going on around you. But remember that as a royal priest, you shall not remain in darkness because your end has been pre-determined by God to show forth His glory.

Other Books

Also By The Author

Step Out

This book encourages you to activate your faith in order to overcome your limitations in life. It outlines in simple but practical terms how you can identify God's power in you to turn around your life for the better. A lot of people believe that it takes special grace to get God's attention. But the good news is that everyone, including you, can access God's presence.

Make a choice to Step Out, Cry Out and Reach Out in faith to our Lord and Saviour Jesus Christ, the 'Author and Finisher' of our faith. As you read this book, it's my prayer that it impacts your thoughts and attitudes positively and lifts you out of the doldrums of fear, intimidation and a poor self-image.

ISBN: 978-1-90797-141-9

Turning The Tide

A sudden rise of a tide would make sailing very difficult. In Exodus 17:11 we see how Moses invoked the power of God on the mountain to win the battle in favour of Israel. You cannot make any headway until you invoke the power of God to turn the tide in your own life.

This book was written to highlight the importance of praying, fasting, studying and invoking the Word and how these can be used as tools for a supernatural turnaround in your circumstances. It is Robert's prayer that as you read this book, the hand of God will change your circumstances to your favour.

ISBN: 978-1-90797-152-5

Available from
www.jesusjoypublishing.co.uk